Presented to:

_____

From:

_____

Living
IN GOD'S GENEROUS DESIGN

Life
WITHOUT
RESERVATION

Life Without Reservation
© 2019 by Michael L. Stickler

ISBN: 978-1-951648-21-3 (paperback)

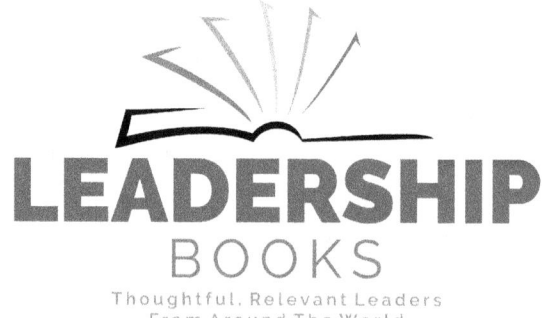

Publisher:
Leadership Books, Inc

Las Vegas, NV – New York, NY

LeadershipBooks.com

Published March 2019
Printed and distributed by Ingram Press

All Rights Reserved. No portion of this book may be reproduced, stored in a retrieval system, or transmitted in any form or by any means-electronic, mechanical, photocopy, recording, scanning, or other-except for brief quotations in critical reviews or articles, without the prior written permission of the publisher.

Unless otherwise indicated, Bible quotations are taken from The Holy Bible: New International Version®. NIV®. Copyright © 1973, 1978, 1984 by Biblica.

Graphic Design:
KAnneDesigns

Dedication:

This book, <u>Life Without Reservation</u>, is dedicated to Art Barkley. Twenty five years ago he took me under his wing to disciple me. He fiercely added to my maturity in Christ.

For his love and encouragement, I am eternally grateful.

~ Mike

From the Author

Most people would think a book is a lonely endeavor. For me, it takes a team. The help of these people have made this work a collaborative effort.

Art Ritter, Executive editor
Steve Wark and **Dave Ficere,** Copy editors
Jerry Brewer, Development editor

Peer Review Team:
Rob Boyland
Dave Bryant
Pastor James Houston-Hencken
Pastor Jay Hull
Pastor Pat Propster
Professor Glenn Sunshine

Life Without Reservation
Living in God's Generous Design
INTRODUCTION

When you hear the word "generosity" you may think of money —or maybe a wealthy philanthropist who gives large sums of it to solve a desperate need. Although using money might be a convenient way to be generous, the Biblical view of "generosity" is something much more than just that – it is an expression of the very nature of God.

Money is just one of the many ways someone can express generosity but living a Life Without Reservation is much more.

Together, we're going to look at the lives of eight people who have lived a life without reservation. As we do so, we'll explore:

- How you can express the heart of God by being generous.
- How generosity is not just an outward act, but also an outflow of the love of God, the Father, for His creation. It's about kindness, mercy, gentleness, forgiveness, reconciliation, and so much more.

Generosity is not about who deserves it or what might be returned to you if you practice generous living. Rather, it comes from a fullness of the soul. Give, knowing it may not be returned. Give, knowing that you have been given in excess of what you can wildly imagine. Give, knowing that you want to be a conduit of His generosity. That kind of giving is where we learn that generosity is essential to Christian discipleship.

This book is not about "the key to health and prosperity." In my view, the idea that we should be generous in order to get something in return is not Biblical generosity. That kind of "giving" actually describes a *quid pro quo* business transaction.

You have made a business deal when you make a payment, barter, or negotiate with the expectation of a return. Nothing is wrong with business transactions. I like business. But it's not giving with a truly pure heart, which is what "giving" and "generosity" are designed to be: an opportunity to give without thought of return, out of gratitude for what we have been given.

Life Without Reservation
TABLE OF CONTENTS

Chapter 1......Generosity is God's Idea..................................1

Chapter 2......We Own Nothing: God Owns *Everything*............19

Chapter 3......Whose Are You?...45

Chapter 4......What is Generosity?...60

Chapter 5......The Idolatry of this Age.....................................79

Chapter 6......Investing in Our Eternity...................................97

Chapter 7......Living a Life Without Reservation....................113

Chapter 8......Having a Vision..133

Chapter 9......Celebrating Generosity.....................................151

Chapter 10......One Last Story..179

What's Next?..184

Chapter 1
GENEROSITY IS GOD'S IDEA

Generosity seems to be popular today. Who doesn't remember Ty Pennington, ABC's *Extreme Home Makeover* host? He encouraged the participants of the show to cry out, "Bus driver, move that bus!" in order to reveal the rehabilitated house given to its owners after a wild week of hammering and painting. On CBS's *Undercover Boss*, employees are given by their boss, the means to achieve the aspirations they shared with a "new employee" – who turns out to have been their boss in disguise. There are philanthropic personalities, like Ellen DeGeneres, Oprah Winfrey, Bill and Melinda Gates, and thousands of others who give of their time and money to improve the lives of others.

Generosity actually dates to the beginning, not to the dawn of civilization but to the dawn of *Creation*. Do you remember Genesis, Chapter 1, verses 1 through 3?

> **Genesis 1:1-3** (NIV)
>
> ¹ In the beginning God created the heavens and the earth. ² Now the earth was formless and empty, darkness was over the surface of the deep, and the Spirit of God was hovering over the waters.
>
> ³ And God said, "Let there be light," and there was light.

God gave the heavens ... and the earth ... and ... light. What? Wait. Don't just read right on past that. He, the Creator of the universe, gave us LIGHT! How important is that? As far as we know, nothing, absolutely *nothing* in all of creation either on earth or in the heavens can live without it! Without light, plants don't grow, without plants, animals die with nothing to eat and there is no oxygen regenerated into the air to breath. Water freezes and nothing survives, including us!

> **"CREATION EXISTS FOR US. HE GAVE IT TO HUMANKIND TO STEWARD AND ENJOY."**

God didn't just end the creation process with light. He also gave us an entire system of life – so complex, that we are only now beginning to unravel its intricacies. He called it CREATION. And He called it "very good."

Creation exists for us. He gave it to humankind to steward and enjoy. (Gen 1:26-30) He first placed Adam in the Garden of Eden, giving him one job, that of tending to the garden. (Gen 2:15) While Adam was tending the garden God created, God concluded that Adam had a need, something Adam never asked for, something he didn't even realize he needed. Why didn't Adam know? Because Adam was content, satisfied with his relationship – this as-yet, unchanged relationship with God. But, being foreknowing (Isa 46:10), God could see his need. It was "not good for man to be alone." (Gen 2:18a) So, He created Eve (Gen 2:21-23) to be a helpmate and companion for Adam. (Gen 2:18b) A gift. A gift Adam didn't even know he needed.

Let's stop here for a moment. If God is foreknowing (and He is), then He knew that giving Eve to Adam would break the pure and undisturbed relationship between just Adam and Himself. Did you read that? He knew where this gift would lead! Even so, He blessed Adam with the gift – which Adam had no inkling of how it would ultimately satisfy him. More so, God, being foreknowing, also knew the outcome with Eve and Adam in the Garden as they would face the temptation that evil would bring them and the consequences they would face because of yielding to it. Having created Adam and Eve with the power to choose between good and evil, He knew they would sin (Rom 8:29; 1 John 3:30; Isa 48:3-5), lose the power to choose good on their own, and now, really rupture that pure and undisturbed relationship with Him for which they were created. Even so, when that finally did happen, when they both ate from the Tree of Knowledge of Good and Evil and their relationship dramatically changed (Gen 3:1-7), He continued to be generous to them.

God's Generous Heart

God is generous, and generosity is both His idea and part of

His nature. You can see His generosity towards His creation even when you mess it up, sin, and misuse your relationship with Him.

FIRST EXAMPLE OF GOD'S GENEROSITY
The Substitution Principle

Let's look back to what happened in the Garden of Eden after Adam and Eve sinned …

Think about it:
- Adam and Eve had a complete, pure and undisturbed relationship with their Creator, signified by their walking together with God in the Garden (Gen 3:8),
- Adam was given one job, to tend God's creation (Gen 2:15) – the Garden,
- Adam was given one rule: Don't eat from the Tree of Knowledge of Good and Evil. (Gen 2:16-17)

Sounds perfect, right? They had no shame, no disappointments, and all their needs were met. Their need to feel acceptance was met by being uniquely created ("formed") by God. (Gen 2:7) Their need for significance was met as they were created in His image. (Gen 1-26-27) Their need to be secure was met through God's provision of the Garden and His endless love. (Gen 22:44; John 3:16; Psa 78:102) The deepest needs of humankind were met by God and by God alone. Even when Adam had a need, one unknown by him, God met it.

But then it happened … man was disobedient against God and suffered the consequences of that action. (Gen 3: 1-7a)

This single action impacts us even to this day. For the first time, humankind had a real rupture in that pure, undisturbed relationship with God. Adam and Eve immediately felt the impact of this disharmony at the moment of their rebellious act: they felt shame (Gen 3:7) and, as a result, they

> **"I TRIED TO HIDE FROM THE CONSEQUENCES OF MY SIN …"**

hid from God. (Gen 3:8-10 Gen 3:8-10) Confronted, they quickly shifted responsibility for their disobedient action (Gen 3:12-13) – Adam to Eve, Eve to the serpent. The serpent even pushed blame onto God! In their shame, they tried to cover themselves – their sin – as signified by donning the leaves. (Gen 3:15)

Sound familiar? I know it does for me. I tried to hide from the consequences of my sin, cast blame elsewhere, and develop an elaborate cover-up. As if the God of the universe can't see through my self-justification ... God saw through Adam's, as well.

The Bible says God went looking for them. (Gen 3:9) This wasn't because God lost them, rather, it was because God felt the disharmony a – the breach – in the pure relationship they had jointly experienced up to the point of their disobedience. Now, they were no longer walking together. Due to the broken relationship, the fulfillment of mankind's deepest needs for significance, acceptance, and security were no longer being sought through a relationship with God. Imagine how this broke God's heart. He created this man and this woman specifically to love and to be loved by Him. He wanted to give us so much yet, because of this one act, we – man and God – experienced disharmony with one another.

I can't comprehend how it must have felt for God, but oh, how this must have broken God's heart! I can remember the brokenness I felt as an earthly father when my sons made willful, frustrating decisions that strained our relationship!

God, being rich in mercy and full of love (Eph 2:4-5) for His children, wanted to restore that pure relationship. He began by providing a more permanent covering for Adam and Eve, but it wasn't cheap. It took the sacrifice of an animal to make clothes for them (Gen 3:21), as the cover for their shame and as payment for their sin. What man could not do for himself, God would provide.

Let's look at this payment thing a bit. Imagine the scene. Here's this little lamb (though the Bible doesn't specify, I imagine a lamb – to be consistent with the imagery we find throughout the rest of scripture). Imagine this lamb peacefully grazing on a grassy meadow within the garden. It's a pleasant day, no predators with which to be concerned. Heck, there hasn't ever been a bad day in the Garden of Eden until this point! Then out of nowhere, a lightning bolt! The Power of God — the Voice of God ... ZAP... turns this peaceful lamb into two pairs of pants and shirts. Wow! Really?! What did the lamb do to deserve this? It was Adam and Eve who broke the one rule. (Gen 3:1-7) It was Adam and Eve who hid and played the blame game in their feeble attempt at covering up their sin. (Gen 3:1-13) Who got the bad end of this deal? That poor little lamb, that's who!

It was the lamb:
- who paid the price of someone else's sin with its life!
- who took on the wrath of God in these two sinner's places.

– and foreshadowed the One:
- who would become the substitute-payer for the sin of mankind.
- who would take on the wrath of God in mankind's sinful place.

Remember, God had given Adam only one rule. He had told Adam that if he ate from that tree he would surely die. (Gen 2:16-17) But instead of immediately taking Adam and Eve's lives in payment for their sin, He gave them a substitute for this payment (at least for the time being) so they could bear their shame in the form of clothing to cover their nakedness. Then, he did even more. He made them a promise while talking to the evil one who had led them to their sin: "(her offspring) will crush your head." (Gen 3:15) It is the final victory over evil that we see in the Son of God's death and resurrection – the final resolution for the sin of humankind when Jesus dies as the payment proffered for humankind's sin – a salvation from that sin that is offered to all humankind – for this original sin and for all of their subsequent sin. He did that so the pure undisturbed fellowship could be restored between God and those who rely on Jesus' sacrifice for their salvation from sin.

A SECOND EXAMPLE OF GOD'S GENEROSITY
The Lamb of God

Another example of God's generosity toward mankind is found in the story of Israel's deliverance from 400 years bondage in Egypt. (Exo 3:7-10)

Even if you have never read the account in the Bible, you may have seen the movie, *The Ten Commandments*. In the story, Moses returned from Midian to Egypt (Exo 4:19-20) in order to follow God's command to tell Pharaoh to: "Let my people go!" (Exo 7:16, Exo 5:1) Moses confronts his stepbrother, the Pharaoh. (Exo 2:10) (Moses had been adopted into the royal family by this Pharaoh's mother when, as a young girl, she had found him in the basket in the river. (Exo 2:3-10) Now in his stepbrother's Egyptian court, Moses gives Pharaoh God's command to release the Israelites.

Pharaoh has an arrogant heart and scoffs at Moses. (Remember, too, the pharaohs believed they were gods.)[1] As a result, different plagues were unleashed upon Egypt – one each time Moses demanded Pharaoh release God's people. (Exo 7:14; 12:32) But each time Pharaoh's heart is further hardened, and he refuses. (Exo 7:13; 14; 8:15; 19,32; 9:7; 37) With each refused demand, God sends a plague to demonstrate HIS power against the false gods of Egypt. In fact, each of the plagues came in direct opposition to one of the many false gods of Egypt. They worshiped the Nile River: God turned it to blood. (Exo 7:14-25) They worshiped the sun: God turned the day into night (Exo 10:21-29) and so forth. Arguably, each plague was more destructive than the previous one.

The last plague was the most devastating of all: the death of the first born of every family in Egypt. (Exo 11:1-10) But God made a provision for His people, as found in Exodus 12. Each Israelite family was to take a spotless lamb, sacrifice it and drain its blood. With the blood, they were to mark the doorframe of the entrance to their home. (Exo 12:1-7) God had instructed Moses that if the blood of the lamb, a perfect lamb, were painted across the doorpost, then all those within that home would be saved. (Exo 12:1-13) This act becomes known as the Passover (Exo 12:14-28), because God promised to "pass His wrath over" (Exo 12:27) each house – including the first-born – sealed with the blood. What they couldn't do to save themselves, God did for them.

If you saw the movie *The Ten Commandments*, you can recall and visualize this particular scene. In the night's sky, fingers of a misty green fog descended from heaven and settled on the ground. Then the fog – representing the death Angel – slowly crept across the ground and seeped under the unmarked doors of each home, those without the blood of the lamb on their doorposts. Across the city, you could hear the rising screams of grief as one first-born after another succumbed to God's wrath. It is sobering to think about the pain of such an experience. (Exo 12:29-30) It is why, even today, Jews celebrate the Passover (Exo 12:14) and their deliverance from God's wrath by the blood of one unblemished lamb. (Exo 12:5-8; 11-13)

---
1   https://www.britannica.com/topic/pharaoh

Now fast-forward in time to the Jordan River. Here is a man, a locust-eating and camel-hair-wearing, crazy man, disheveled and unkempt, by most accounts – named John the Baptist. (Mark 1:1-11; Matt 3:1-13) Jesus approaches

> "HERE IS A MAN, A LOCUST-EATING AND CAMEL-HAIR-WEARING, CRAZY MAN, DISHEVELED AND UNKEMPT, BY MOST ACCOUNTS - NAMED JOHN THE BAPTIST."

him and wants to be baptized. What does John say – knowing that the religious elite, the Pharisees, are watching, listening, and ridiculing? He declares: "Behold, the Lamb of God who takes away the sins of the world." (John 1:29) Why would he say that, using those words and unnecessarily offending these religious leaders? Unless, of course, he was making the boldest of statements.

John knew that in Jesus, mankind would be reconciled to God. (Rom 5:10-16) Only through Jesus, and no other, the wrath of God would be quenched and the harmony of a pure relationship with God the Father would be restored once and for all. (Rom 5:10-19; Heb 9:26; 10:12-14) We could now have through Christ, the same relationship with God that Adam and Eve had before their disobedience. (Rom 5:17-21) John was declaring that Jesus was our final, complete substitution. There need be – there can be – no other. Through Jesus Christ, the old covenant would pass; the New Covenant of Grace would be established (Heb 8:13). Through Christ, we all could be adopted as children of God. (Rom 8:15; Eph 1:5)

With these words, John declared that there was nothing we could do to make ourselves acceptable to God. Through His death and burial, this Lamb paid our sin debt. It was only what someone else – the perfect and sinless One – did that made us acceptable to God for fellowship with Him. Jesus, the Son of God (Eph 2:4-22), through His death, burial, and resurrection, finished the work of the Father (John 17:1-5), so that we could be reconciled to God. (1Pet 1:3-9; 1 John 4:8-10)

THE THIRD EXAMPLE

Let's go back to the Nation of Israel as recorded in Exodus 19. Remember when Moses went up Mount Sinai to meet with God and receive the Law? He was gone 40 days. (Exo 32; 34:28) In his absence, the people in the camp became restless, filled with worry, and even frightened. Why? They had become accustomed to being led by the Pillar and the Cloud. (Exo 13:21-22) They relied on Moses to be their intermediary (Exo 20:18-22; 33:7-11), to tell them God's will every step of the way. (Exo 20:22) God had become accessible, not just to the Jewish patriarchs and matriarchs; but, to every member of the nation. The Almighty Creator God had softened His voice, hid His glory within a cloud, and made His very infinite nature finite, to be seen, felt, and heard by His people in the desert. (Exo 20:18-22) This was majestic and mysterious stuff. Imagine being delivered out of bondage, out of the hands of the mightiest power on Earth, then being led and fed by the very Hand of God. (Exo 16:35; Exo 13:21-22) Now suddenly, God and Moses are missing. Can you relate? I can.

There are times when I have those 'mountaintop experiences' where the Holy Spirit feels tangibly involved in every detail of my life. Then, other times he's distant, seemingly abandoning me on a cold winter's day, His presence nowhere to be found. It's during those times – the more difficult times – that I need to know and believe by faith that He will return to me. But, how do I experience God's presence in the mountains *and* in the valleys – during the spiritually warm summers and spiritually cold winters of life? I think that we, in part, find the answer at the foot of Mount Sinai. There, in the Tent of Meeting, just outside of the camp of the Nation of Israel, God said to Moses, "Tell the Israelites to take for Me a contribution. You are to receive the contribution for Me from everyone whose heart prompts them to give." So, Moses did. (Exo 35:4-29)

One of the best ways to enjoy your salvation here on earth and to return to God's presence and live a life without reservation is to give. You know the wonderful feeling you get when you give? The very act of giving comes from, or leads us to, the understanding that all is God's anyway, including us, ourselves.

> **"ONE OF THE BEST WAYS TO LIVE A LIFE WITHOUT RESERVATION IS TO GIVE."**

(1 Cor 3:16; 6:19-20) Think about how counter-intuitive this idea is.

When things are the hardest, when our resources seem to be drying up, when God seems the furthest from us, we should give! (Mark 12:44; Luke 21:3-4) We should not isolate, not hold on tighter, not guard our savings, and not become more self-sufficient and self-absorbed. Instead, God says to give thanks with an act of gratitude

(Phil 4:1-20), knowing that He gave us life, the very air we breathe, our very next breath, and all of creation. (Ps 8:3; 24:1-2) He is the artist and we are His canvas, from which He intends to make a masterpiece. That is what we have to be thankful for!

Consider this: In Exodus 25, God instructed the Israelites to build a sanctuary for Him. (Exo 25; 27:19) He gave them specific, detailed instructions on how this structure would be built, where His very presence could rest. (Exo 25-27:19) The blueprints seemed extremely elaborate and, to the common man, might appear that God required grandiose surroundings in which to dwell.

But, that's not the idea here. You see, it wasn't merely the quality of the wood, metals, or drapes. Nor was it simply the sparkle or clarity or carats of the jewels on the breastplate of the high priest, nor the purity or rare value of the gold overlaid upon the ark. It wasn't the brilliant architectural design with the aroma of sacrifices and frankincense to create the aura and ambiance to draw God's presence. (Exo 28 - Exo 30) But here, with even more significance than those truths, is the wonderful revelation:

> ... that God's house was built
> out of the "GIFTS"
> of "everyone whose HEART
> prompted them to GIVE."
> (Exo 35:5, 21, 22, 29; 25:2)

God's people voluntarily returned to God those things that were His anyway, out of a heart of gratitude, giving to one another and to this Holiest of causes. Now that's a place where God's presence can rest. Although God doesn't dwell any longer in houses of wood and stone (Acts 17:24-31); nevertheless, His presence today continues to live on in those whose hearts are generous towards Him – as we read in Jeremiah, Chapter 31, verses 31 to 33.

Generous Grace

Another gift of grace (Rom 5:12-16) from a generous God gives us victory in this life over the power of sin. (Rom 5:12-6:11) This gift – through Jesus' resurrection – was nothing we earned or deserved. (Eph 2:8-9)

John 3:16 (NIV)
> For God so loved the world that He GAVE His only begotten Son, that whosoever believes in Him should not perish, but have eternal life.

Through this gift of grace, you have been saved! (Eph 2:8-9) Not because of anything you did, it was a gift from a generous God. (Eph 1:18)

Generosity – as part of living a life without reservation – was God's idea!

Often, we confuse mercy and grace. I find it easy to define them this way:
- Mercy is *not* getting something <u>bad</u> that you deserve.
- Grace is getting something <u>good</u> you don't deserve or ever earned. (Eph 2:8-9)

I enjoy telling this next story, which illustrates the differences mercy and grace:

Years ago, I worked for a company located about 30 miles north of my home. One of the unbreakable policies of working there was that you be at your desk ready to work at 8:00 am sharp. I was a young man, with a young family who was just learning how to juggle all my responsibilities. Particularly challenging was budgeting enough time in the morning to be at work on time.

One specific week was especially hectic. On Monday, I didn't leave my house until 7:30 am. Of course, I tried to make up time by speeding up the freeway. Taking the off-ramp to exit, I took the right corner way too fast and immediately found that I had entered a school zone with a 15-mph limit. On my right, was the middle school and on my left, was a police sub-station. I glanced down at my speedometer; I was doing 35-mph! I held my breath and maintained that speed through the school zone and the remaining miles to my workplace. After parking quickly, I ran through the lot and burst into the office where I threw myself into my chair, only five minutes late. My boss was on the phone and I seemed to make it without notice. I breathed a sigh of relief.

Tuesday morning was worse. My son had missed his ride and was about to miss the school bus if I didn't get him to the bus stop.

Chapter 1: Generosity is God's Idea

The race was on! With a lot of scrambling and vocal encouragement (otherwise known as yelling), I dropped my son at the bus and hit the freeway at 7:35 am. As I sped along the freeway toward work, I kept checking my rearview mirror watching for the Highway Patrol. As I approached my exit, I was so busy looking behind me I misjudged the exit, my speed, and the curve – completely forgetting the school zone. This time I was doing *40*-mph and a shiny police car was just turning out of the parking lot on my left and into the lane next to me. I knew I was in trouble as I sped past the patrol car. There was nothing I could do but throw up a "help me" prayer, as I knew what would happen next.

    Sure enough, he lit up his light bar and moved in right behind me. Next, I did something amusing. I slowed down, turned on my blinker, and slowly pulled over to the right. All of a sudden, I was "Mr. Safe Driver." The entire process took me another quarter of a mile. There I sat, waiting, as the officer took his time to step out of his car and walk forward to mine. I rolled down my window as this large, professional officer, exuding authority said, "License and registration, please." I handed him my papers and he walked back to his car. The whole time I'm praying, "Don't take me to jail, don't take me to jail." Finally, with what felt like forever, he walked back up to my window. He bent down and said, "Mr. Stickler, do you know why I stopped you today?" But, before I could respond, his radio crackled and I heard a woman's voice and a bunch of gibberish. The officer became immediately distracted while listening, then he tossed my license and registration through the window and onto my lap. "Don't do it again," he said sternly and briskly walked back to his car, started the engine and drove off with his lights flashing and siren blaring. Stunned, I sat there in silence! I arrived at my desk twenty minutes late. My boss asked me why I was late and I told him what had just happened.

    He did not find it humorous.

    Wednesday morning rolls along and, as I was reaching to turn the knob of the front door (and on time), my beloved wife began a conversation with me. It was one of those conversations you don't want to have at all, let alone when you are about to leave on time.

But I could tell it was something she needed to discuss, right now, at this moment. It was emotionally charged and of deep importance to her. My other son was failing a class! Patiently I listened and tried to produce a swift resolution without appearing too distracted. It didn't work. She could see that I wasn't really listening. Along with not listening, I was not validating her concern. Of course, she wanted to know why I was distracted and not enthusiastically listening, which led her to ask some probing questions. I had to disclose about being late to work and my boss' concern. That led to the question, "Why were you 20 minutes late?" Oh gosh, now I needed to divulge all of the prior day's events. My son missing his ride, more questions; my choosing to speed, more concerned questions; my being pulled over by the police, more deeply concerning questions and a few remarks like "through a school zone? Really Mike!" I followed up by a sheepish, "I know, I know." All this burned up time and the more it went on, the more I felt like I was sinking in quicksand. Finally, I left the house at 7:40 am. Yep, you see where this is going.

Late again, I raced up the freeway, took the off-ramp on two wheels, and hit the school zone at 45 miles per hour. And, yes, encountered the *same* cop on the *same* stretch of road, all just a few hundred feet from my office parking lot.

He stopped me. "Aren't you the same guy from yesterday?" he exclaimed. "Give me your license and registration." As I did, I kept my mouth shut.

A few minutes later, I had a $500 ticket in my hand. Not much else was exchanged between us, but I could feel his regret that he hadn't cited me the day before. By the time I was free to go, I was 30 minutes late to work. My boss called me into his office. After a short, but direct, reprimand, I returned to my work with a written warning in my personnel file.

Waking up early Thursday morning, I had no intention of being late again. The night before we had attended church and the family potluck. Because of that outing, I didn't have a chance to talk to my wife about what happened Wednesday morning. After a quick shower, I settled in at the breakfast table with my coffee and the newspaper. The house was awake. I could hear my boys rustling around, as they readied for school. My wife came to sit with me for her coffee and morning cereal. Then came the question I dreaded; "How's it going at work? Any added fallout from being late?" With that question, I answered with the tale of the previous mornings' events.

She just sat in stunned silence as I recounted the details including the citation and reprimand. All she could say was, "You know we can't afford $500 for your ticket. We certainly can't afford for you to lose your job either." With empathy in her eyes, she took my hand and prayed. I wiped my eyes, feeling very defeated, mumbled my good-byes and headed to the car.

As I started the engine, the digital clock lit up: 7:45 am. "No, that can't be right! I woke up early!" I had lost track of time. Off to the races I went, heading up the freeway at more than 80 mph. This time I was determined not to be late, my resolve rooted more in fear of the consequences than in reality. If I hadn't let fear override my common sense, I would have accepted I was already too late to be on time for work. Approaching my off-ramp, I pushed the limit of my car's cornering ability and was a mere blur as I sped through the school zone at 50+ mph.

Just as happened previously, the same policeman was entering into the left lane. I hit the brakes hard almost skidding. It didn't matter. He pulled in right behind me and turned on his lights. This time the siren came on. I made it safely to the right shoulder and waited, dreading what was going to happen next. This time the officer moved swiftly with much more purpose. "Three days in a row?? Out of the car!" he ordered. He moved me to the front of my car and, with a painful thud, pushed my upper body and face on to the hood. "Put your hands behind your back," he ordered. Humiliated, I said nothing as the cold steel of the handcuffs unbearably tightened around my wrists. With a tug I was off the hood, stumbling as he pushed me over to the police car. As I was stuffed into the back seat, he declared, "You are under arrest." The door slammed shut.

Even though the distance was short, the drive to the courthouse was long. All I could think about was my job. My head was swimming with a myriad of thoughts. I would lose my job. My wife would be angry and disappointed. My car would be impounded. My bank account would be drained. My life was about to change.

Deeply ashamed, I was escorted into the courtroom. I couldn't

LIFE WITHOUT RESERVATION

help but notice that as the court was called to order it even seemed everyone was waiting on me. The bailiff took my arm, walked me to a chair and sat me down. The judge acknowledged the officer who brought me in.

"Good morning, son," the judge said warmly.

The officer nodded his head. I thought to myself, the cop is the judge's son? This isn't going to go well.

The judge: "What's the charge?"

The officer: "Mr. Stickler here was clocked going 35 miles per hour over the speed limit in a school zone."

The judge: "Anything else?"

The officer: "Your honor, in the two previous days, Tuesday and Wednesday, Mr. Stickler was stopped for speeding in the same school zone, traveling in excess of 20 miles per hour over the limit. Yesterday, I issued him a citation."

The judge: Raising his eyes over the papers he was reading. "Mr. Stickler, is this true?"

Me: "Don't I get a lawyer or something?"

The judge: "Yes, you do. Officer, I am appointing you Mr. Stickler's attorney."

The officer/now attorney: "Your honor, Mr. Stickler pleads guilty, because he is guilty."

The judge: "Is that true, Mr. Stickler?"

Me (meekly), "Yes."

The judge: "Then, as the law requires, I sentence you to one year in jail and a $10,000 fine."

The sound of the gavel slamming down was all I heard next.

The officer/attorney: "Your honor, respectfully, that is an extremely harsh sentence."

The judge: "Maybe so, but justice demands it. As a righteous judge, I must punish those who break the law."

After a long contemplative pause, the officer/attorney: "Your honor, how about I take the penalty for Mr. Stickler? I will pay his fine and serve his one-year sentence."

The judge: "Son, are you sure you want to do that?"

The officer/attorney: "Well, I would prefer if something else be worked out, but I am willing."

Chapter 1: Generosity is God's Idea

The judge: "Unfortunately, there is nothing else I can do. My law is perfect and demands justice. Mr. Stickler, are you willing to accept this generous offer?"

Me: "Why would he do that? ... I am guilty ... who would do such a thing?"

The judge, with authority: "Mr. Stickler! Do you accept his paying your penalty for your crime?"

Me (muttering and still not understanding), "I do." I was quite astonished.

The judge: "Then I sentence the officer to pay the just penalty owed by Michael Stickler, to serve one year in jail and pay $10,000 fine forthwith. Bailiff, remand the officer to jail. The Court is adjourned and justice is served."

The bailiff walked over to me and removed my handcuffs. Then, he walked over to the officer/attorney, placed the cuffs on his wrists and guided him across the courtroom and through a door. As they entered together, the officer/attorney looked at me one last time and smiled.

Let me ask you the same questions as if that had happened to you: How would you feel about the officer? What would you do?

I have shared this story to several hundred people over the years. Here are some of the more common and memorable responses:

"I would be profoundly grateful."

"I would go to the jail every day to visit him."

"Stunned at first, then I would mow his lawn and wash his car every day for the rest of his life."

A prisoner in California said, "I would put money on his books," referring to his jail commissary account, which allows an inmate to buy a few extras while incarcerated.

One young man said, "I wouldn't be a chump and forget about him. I would be there to pick him up the day he was released. I would care for him, let him live with me, whatever he needed or required."

This story, though fictional, does tell of God's gift of grace for you and me. Take a moment to read these verses:

Ephesians 2:1-10 (NIV)

> [1-3] As for you, you were dead in your transgressions and sins, in which you used to live when you followed the ways of this world and of the ruler of the kingdom of the air, the spirit who is now at work in those who are disobedient. All of us also lived among them at one time, gratifying the cravings of our flesh and following its desires and thoughts. Like the rest, we were by nature deserving of wrath.
>
> [4-7] But, because of His great love for us, God, who is rich in mercy, made us alive with Christ even when we were dead in transgressions – it is by grace you have been saved. And God raised us up with Christ and seated us with Him in the heavenly realms in Christ Jesus, in order that in the coming ages He might show the incomparable riches of His grace, expressed in His kindness to us in Christ Jesus.
>
> [8-10] For it is by grace you have been saved, through faith-and this is not from yourselves, it is the gift of God – not by works, so that no one can boast. For we are God's handiwork, created in Christ Jesus to do good works, which God prepared in advance for us to do.

The *fictional* story of the speeding ticket is another demonstration of what Jesus ACTUALLY DID for you and me. Let's see how it lines up – and review the week's activities in the story.

Monday: I was lost in my own selfish desires. (Eph 2:1-3)

Tuesday: I am not given a ticket, which I deserve. Mercy. I remain free. (Eph 2:4)

Wednesday: With the promise of justice, instead of going to jail, I am given something I don't deserve: Grace instead of justice. Though the law demanded justice, I was given the gift of grace through the offering of the officer/attorney who paid the penalty of my crime. (Eph 2:7)

Thursday and following: Notice the responses people have given me over the years as well as your own response. When we experience such grace, grace that humbles, and atones, it produces generosity and gratitude! This is something God created before the beginning of time. (Eph 2:8-10)

Grace doesn't breed license to sin, to be greedy, or to be indulgent of our desires. This gift of grace produces amazing, extraordinary generosity in ordinary people. Do you see it?

God's profound generosity is what sets Christianity apart from all other religions or belief systems. It's a realization that you and I are in deep need of acceptance, significance, and security with our Creator God. Being as just as He is, He responds to our need by giving us this incredible and extravagantly generous grace to restore us – to fulfill our need – and to have eternal fellowship with Him. He has already paid the way for it – not because we deserve it – but because of His infinite love for us.

Chapter 2

WE OWN NOTHING: GOD OWNS *EVERYTHING*

Years ago, my wife and I were on vacation at Niagara Falls. While enjoying the day admiring God's beautiful creation, we noticed a crowd beginning to gather nearby. We wandered over to see if maybe there was a street performer or musician about to perform. To our astonishment, we saw a tightrope stretched across the entire width of the falls. There stood a man – the Great Waldo – a famous tightrope walker about to begin his greatest accomplishment. He was attempting to walk across the falls, risking certain death on a tightrope.

As the crowd began to build, the TV cameras pressed in on the Great Waldo as he stepped to the stage and took the microphone. "Welcome everyone, thank you for coming out today to see the greatest most perilous attempt to walk a tightrope in human history."

The audience cheered and applauded.

"I have spent my life pursuing the greatest challenges of balance and concentration. I began at a young age," he said while pointing to a large photo of himself as a young child walking on a tightrope five or six feet off the ground. "Over the years, I have gotten better and better." Again, he pointed to a collection of photos detailing more and more riskier situations. These photos depicted him precariously crossing between two Manhattan skyscrapers, between the expanse of a bridge, and one that appeared to be over the Grand Canyon. "Today will be my last and greatest walk. Today, I will cross the mighty Niagara Falls. One and a half miles across, the wind is gusting up to 40 miles per hour and I have approximately 10 hours to complete my journey before nightfall."

The crowd erupted with applause.

"The risk is high. If I make one misstep in that one and a half miles, or if the wind exceeds 45 miles per hour, I will fall to a certain death over the falls." The crowd hushed. "I must complete the walk before nightfall. Once I lose the light, I will not be able to go further. I will be unable to see the rope – or have any depth perception to see even the slightest movement of the rope in relationship to my body. I literally will not be able to tell which way is up or which way is down."

There was stillness in the crowd. You could have heard a pin drop.

"There will be NO rescue! No one in the world is qualified to come out on this wire – but me. A helicopter rescue is futile. The wind makes it impossible to lower a rescuer. And, the downdraft of the rotor wash from the helicopter will likely blow me off the wire long before a rescuer could be lowered."

The crowd now appeared concerned that maybe this might possibly be a spectacle of seeing his death.

He shouted, "What do you think, can I do it?"

Applause broke the silence.

"Is today the day that I will break the record?" he shouted.

The crowd became more and more convinced and now earnestly applauded and cheered.

Then the Great Waldo looked right at me. I had been in the front row, so I could easily be called upon. "You, sir, do you believe that I can complete this incredible record-breaking feat?"

I responded, "Sure."

"Sir, do you trust that against all odds, within the next ten hours I will be safe on the other side of the falls having completed this record-breaking feat of balance and human will?"

"Yes, I see that you have successfully done all of these other amazing tightrope walks. I trust you can do this one, too!" I chirped.

"Do you really believe I can do it?"

"YES!" I cheered.

"Do you really have the trust in me I will complete this journey?"

"Yes. I do. You can do it!" I was clapping now.

And so was the crowd. In fact, a long, sustained applause erupted amid the cheers and encouragements. While the crowd cheered and clapped, the Great Waldo reached behind the stage where he stood, lifted up a wheelbarrow and placed it on the right rope, then jumped up on the rope himself. The crowd's applause began to wane in anticipation that he was about to begin his walk over Niagara Falls.

> **"GET IN THIS WHEELBARROW AND RIDE ..."**

But instead he paused, looked right down at me and took a microphone and quietly said: "Sir, do you still trust that I can do this?"

"Yes," I answered ... but, much more tentatively this time.
"Then, get in this wheelbarrow and ride with me across."

Believing vs. Trusting

The apostle Paul said, "If you confess with your mouth the Lord Jesus and believe in your heart that God has raised Him from the dead, you will be saved." (Rom 10:9-10)

The idea of Biblical belief contains a component of trust. It's not just a conceptual belief that it happened. It's more than that. It's trusting that it has happened, will happen, and is happening in your life now.[1] How do you have belief like that? By faith in Jesus, the Christ.[2]

Relate back to my (OK – again, fictional) story about the Great Waldo. I believed that he could do this mind-blowing feat of walking across Niagara Falls on the tightrope, even against all reason or likelihood of success. I based that belief on what he had done in the past, weighing all his other accomplishments. That little bit of knowledge of who he was and what he had done helped me cross that threshold from doubt to belief. That alone, however, is not what God has called you to. He has called you to a 'wheelbarrow' trust.

It's not enough for the Christian to believe that Jesus died for you once, a long time ago. God's asking you to trust Him with your life, to 'get in and ride' – just like the story. It's a risk, sometimes a BIG risk. But that is where faith comes in. NOT faith in your talents – for what special skill or ability do you have for a death-defying wheelbarrow ride? NOT faith in yourself – for what do you offer in the wheelbarrow ride? It's faith solely in the Master of tightrope walking. It's faith in *His* skills, *His* abilities, *His* character.

> **"GOD'S ASKING YOU TO TRUST HIM WITH YOUR LIFE."**

You might say, "Mike, that is such a risk, who would do it?" My friend, without a perceived risk, you don't need faith – although God will give you that, too. He promised you He would provide you the faith you need, by His grace, in every situation with which you are presented. All you need to do to claim it for yourself is to be willing to have Him as the Lord (owner) of your life. A relationship with you, by the way, that He already has.

God has ownership of your entire life. He made you. He bought you. He paid for your sins through the sacrifice of the precious blood of His son, Jesus. This is the sin you were born into, and it includes the sin of your rebellious disobedience through the time you became a Christian and continues even through today. His sacrificial shedding of His precious blood continues as a payment until you die. Even if you try to usurp His rightful ownership of your life, you can't. You are no longer your own. You are His!

Releasing the grip on your perception of ownership over your life by faith and trusting Him with it will be the most rewarding decision of faith you can ever make. But we really don't like to let go, do we? Not completely. We often think we have surrendered everything until we are required to trust him further, trust him with something that is riskier than ever before. Often, we choose not to allow the Lord access to all of who we are, what we possess or understand, or what we do or choose to leave undone. We say, "I have given you all I can; but, not this," or we say, "I know the Bible teaches this, but I just don't believe it … or I don't want to believe it." We say, "I know the Holy Spirit wants to change me in this way; but, I like, or am comfortable with how I am now and what I am doing now." These little dialogues are signs that we are usurping the Lord's ownership in our lives. It leads to dissatisfaction and complaining in a life that should be full of generosity, contentment, and complete satisfaction.

Israel's Journey

Let me illustrate my point with the nation of Israel. You can follow along in the **Figure 2-1. Overview of the Israelite Journey** timeline.

Israel's timeline:

1. Bondage

The nation of Israel was in bondage to, (Exo 3 – 11) captive in, and dependent on Egypt for 400 years. (Exo 3:7-8a) Though they cried out to God, their existence was dependent upon Egyptian law, provision, forced slavery, and the Pharaoh's whim. (Deut 6:23)

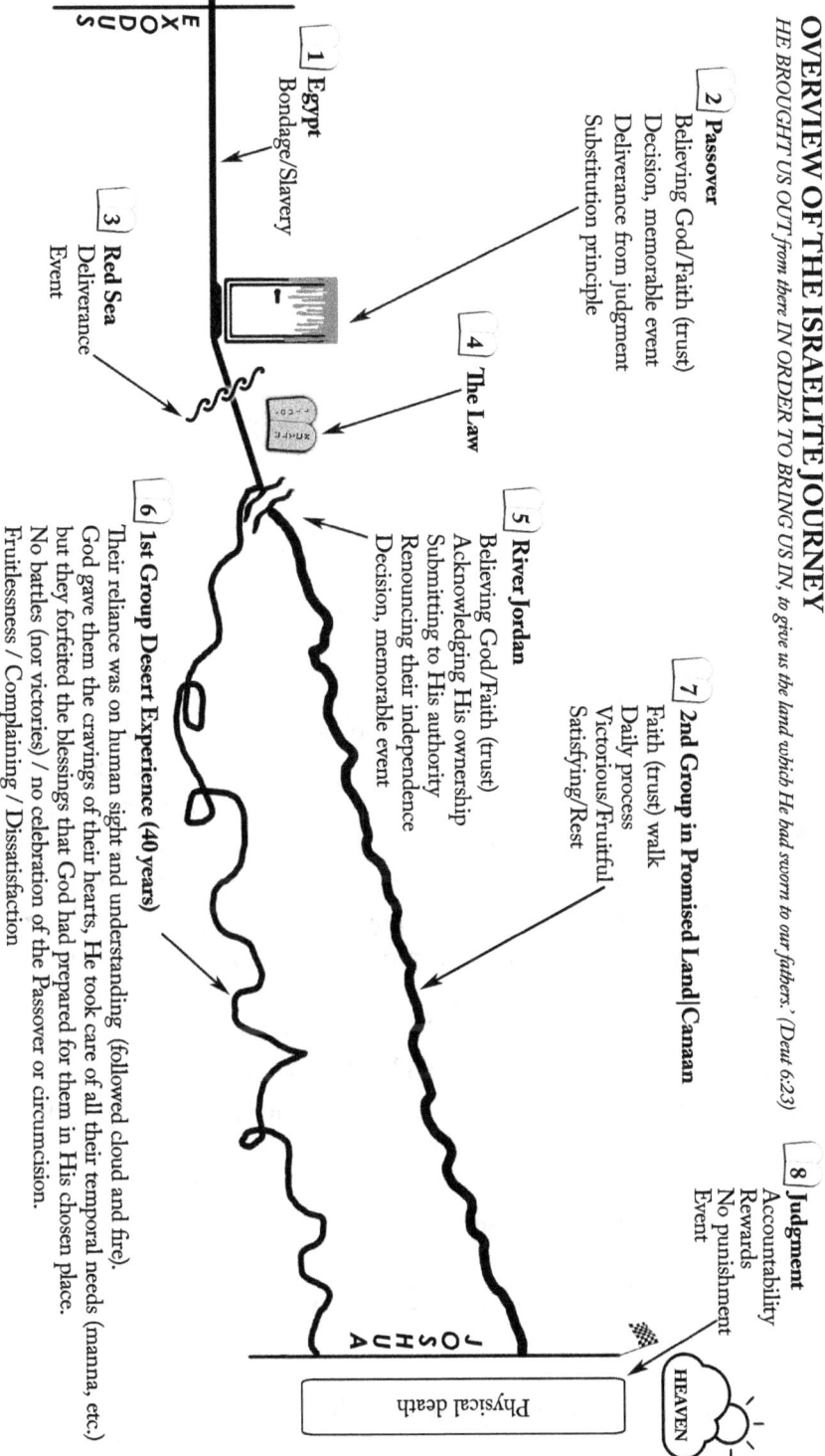

Figure 2-1

2. God provided Israel a Deliverer

God sends Moses – Israel's deliverer to demand Egypt's ruler, Pharaoh, to release the Nation of Israel from their bondage. But Pharaoh refused. With each refusal, God sent a plague upon Egypt to soften Pharaoh's hard heart and release the captives. As I mentioned in Chapter 1, each plague was an attack on Egypt's source of perceived power from one of their gods. He infested Egypt with locust, an affront to Min, one of Egypt's gods. He turned the Nile River to blood, an affront to Hapi, the Nile River god. In all, the God of Israel brought ten plagues upon Egypt. The final plague was the death of every firstborn in Egypt.

God provides an escape for those who trust Him!

God provides Israel, through Moses, a clear path to avoid His wrath and the death of their firstborn. By trust, each household of Israel is to sacrifice a perfect, unblemished lamb and the blood of the lamb is to be applied to the lintel and doorposts of the front door to their house. Moses instructs that those of each house who follow this procedure will be spared this terrible plague, as the angel of death will literally 'pass over' that household. After the previous plagues, this last judgment of God broke the will of Pharaoh and the Egyptian people, whereby he relented, allowing Israel to be released from their bondage. But, even more than that they were released with all the wealth they had created during the 430 years they had lived in Egypt and the treasure they had asked of the Egyptians as they were leaving which included wagons of gold and jewels. Egypt was only too glad to get rid of them, and quickly! To gain a better understanding of the context of how epic this exit was read Exodus 1:1-14 and then go to Exodus 12:31-42. From that day forward, Egypt no longer had any literal power over Israel!

God's people: Most scholars estimate nearly two million people left Egypt with Moses – accounting for the six hundred thousand men on foot, plus the women and children in their families and the many others who went with them, as reported in Exodus 12:37–38. This was a nation of significant size and threat to Egypt.

3. The First Water Experience: The Red Sea

As Moses leads God's people out of Egypt, He brings them to

the Red Sea. At the shore they make camp and Moses waits for God's direction. Meanwhile, back in Egypt, Pharaoh changes his mind and his heart returns to its hardened condition. He calls upon his army to chase down the Israelites and destroy them.

Do you remember watching the movie, *The Ten Commandments*? Pharaoh, played by Yul Brenner, rides to the top of a mountain over-looking the Red Sea and sees the Jewish encampment. As his horse rears up and his chariot stops, he says to his driver, "The God of Moses is a poor general!" referring to what appeared to be a boxed-in situation for the nation of Israel, with their backs to the sea and no apparent way of escape. At full gallop, the Egyptian army comes barreling down the mountain, spears drawn in preparation to wipe out all the men, women and children of Israel. But God intervenes. He places a wall of fire between Pharaoh's army and God's people and then parts the Red Sea. Moses leads the nation of Israel through the divided waters to dry land.

Now take a moment and imagine this scene. There is a wall of fire on one side and two walls of water as the Israelites pass through the sea to a new life. Think about Pharaoh's viewpoint. The God of the universe has just given his prey time, by the wall of fire and the ability to escape through the parting sea. Just a few moments ago, Pharaoh thought Israel was his to destroy. Now he is the one trapped, unable to move forward as he watches millions of people, animals, and the treasures of Egypt escape by the Hand of God.

What's Pharaoh's response? He sends his army after Israel, as soon as the wall of fire subsides. Then he orders a chase into the still-parted Red Sea. Who is the "poor general" now? As the entire Egyptian army is committed into the parted sea, God releases His hold on the waters and the army is completely destroyed: man, horse, and chariot. Historically factual, after the loss of Egypt's financial wealth, the loss of its army, and the devastation of the plagues, Egypt never recovered or returned to the world power it once was (Eze 29:1-15, 29-32; Isa 20; Jer 46). On the other hand, the nation of Israel was delivered from bondage, delivered from Egypt's influence, and delivered from its power. They were now free to live the life God had intended for them.

4. God makes His will known to Israel

From Egypt, Moses leads Israel to Mt. Sinai to receive God's Law. Leaving God's people at the bottom of the mountain, Moses ascends and remains for forty days. While Moses is away, many of the people become impatient, disheartened, and discouraged. In just forty days, they turned back to their old "Egyptian" ways of living. The Bible describes drunkenness, wanton sexuality, and more. The people even fashion an idol in the form of a golden calf to go before them as they consider returning to Egypt.

Let's recap what they have lived through and seen up to this point:

- God brought ten plagues upon the most powerful nation on the earth to deliver them from bondage.
- God provided a wall of fire to protect them from Pharaoh and his army.
- God parted the Red Sea to provide a way of escape from Pharaoh's revenging army, ultimately destroying that very army.

The irony here is that Israel was going to do to themselves the very thing that the powerful army of Egypt could not do to them. After all God had done for them to get them to the foot of Mt. Sinai, they were prepared to turn their back on Him, take their wealth, and willingly go back to be enslaved by Egypt!

On Mt. Sinai, God reveals His will to Moses. God's own finger writes His Ten Commandments upon two stone tablets. When Moses returns to Israel at the bottom of the mountain, he discovers their wanton disrespectfulness towards God and throws the Ten Commandment tablets on the ground before the disobedient. Each disobedient person is slain — they literally died with the Law of God at their feet.

5. Second Water Experience: The Jordan River

All this time, God led Israel by a pillar of fire and a cloud. By day, the cloud that went before them guided the way across the desert and provided shade from the sun. By night, a pillar of fire provided direction, light, and warmth. Through this method, the Lord God led His people to the Jordan River. Once there, He instructed His people, through Moses, to cross the river Jordan into the land He had promised their forefathers – the Promised Land – a land of milk and honey, overflowing with everything God's people would need. What did Israel do? They sought proof that if this was the land in which they would settle. They wanted to be sure it was all that God had promised! As such, they sent spies over the Jordan to scope out the land and then report back on what they found. When the spies returned, they reported it was all that God had promised. They had found it to be a truly beautiful land, and one filled with milk and honey. There was only one issue. The inhabitants of the land were mighty – GIANTS and Israel's soldiers were like the grasshoppers compared to these descendants of the Nephilim. Because of this discovery, Israel refused to trust God and cross over into the Promised Land.

Now, let's pause here for a moment.

These are the same people who:
- by the Hand of God were delivered out of their bondage in Egypt,
- had lived through the ten plagues of God,
- had in their possession the treasures of Egypt, and
- had passed through the parted Red Sea while God held back their enemy Egypt with a wall of fire.

God had:
- provided for them in the trek across the desert,
- led them by a pillar and a cloud,
- given them His law on Mt. Sinai and destroyed those who rebelled, and
- had bestowed many other miracles upon Israel reported in the Bible which I have chosen not to chronicle here.

Yet, these same people could not trust God and receive His promise.

With all they had seen and experienced, you'd think they would have easily trusted God's promise. But they did not.

6. Desert Living: Complaining and Dissatisfaction

So, God led them back into the desert. For forty years they

wandered, continuing to be led by the pillar and cloud. God met Israel's every need, providing food – manna – from heaven, and water where there was no lake or river. Their clothes never wore out and their sandals never wore down. When they complained about the manna, God gave them meat. Israel's reliance was on human sight and understanding (following the cloud and fire). God gave them the cravings of their hearts. He took care of all their temporal needs (manna, *etc*.) but they forfeited the blessing that God had prepared for Israel in His chosen place. While in the desert they wandered with no direction, often crossing the same ground over and over, literally wandering in circles. In the desert they had no battles but they also enjoyed no victories. While in the desert, they had no celebrations, either of the Passover or circumcision. For forty years the Israelite's lives were branded with fruitlessness, complaining, and dissatisfaction.

7. The Promised Land

After 40 years of wandering through the desert, the Nation of Israel returned again to the edge of the Jordan River, across from the Promised Land. Once again He told them to cross the river and receive the land that He had promised their forefathers – a land of milk and honey– (abundant provision) promising that everywhere their foot shall tread, He will give them victory.

So, what did they do? They *again* sent spies over to check out this Promised Land. This time, however, a key fortress city called Jericho was blocking their entry just beyond the river. These spies, sent to check out Jericho's might, found a way to sneak into the city where they met a woman named Rahab. Rahab had a distinctive occupation … she was a prostitute. But apparently, she was one who kept her ears open and had a keen memory.

Right off the bat, she said to them, "Where have you been?"

The spies confused and a bit stunned, respond, "What do you mean?"

> **"WHERE HAVE YOU BEEN?"**

"I know who you are," continued Rahab, "you're the chosen of God. We heard how your God goes before you. How He delivered you from Egypt. How He parted the Red Sea to deliver you from your adversary. Forty years ago, we heard you were at the other side of the Jordan River and our hearts melted with fear as we laid down our swords and waited for you to come take our city. But you never came. Where have you been?"

Can you imagine if you were one of the Israelites? You might be thinking, "If we had just trusted God, all the pain of the last 40 years could have been avoided!"

Word got out that the Israelites were in Jericho and the city guards were looking for them. Knowing this, Rahab hid them on the roof of her house and then lowered them down the city walls to escape. But before the spies escaped, they agreed to protect Rahab and her household when they returned to conquer the city. The spies followed her plan and directions to return to the Israelite encampment where they reported all that they discovered in the Promised Land. They reported, as before, there was a terrible fortress city with a mighty army, but it was clear God had delivered it into their hands. All they needed to do was trust God and cross the Jordan River, entering into the life God always wanted for them. This time they trusted God and crossed the Jordan River into the land God had promised them and their forefathers.

Once they crossed over, some interesting changes happened. The pillar and cloud stopped leading them. Their clothes began to show wear, and manna stopped falling on the ground each morning. Because they were in the place God desired for them, trusting Him wholeheartedly, God provided all they needed, more than what they could have imagined. They didn't need to ask God for every little provision or direction for their lives. It was already provided for them as a by-product of being in the Promised Land. They also now were faced with battles. Remember, Israel did not have an experienced army and had not experienced a battle in 40 years. But they were given every place their feet would tread.

So, how would they conquer the city of Jericho, a city with 20-foot thick[170] walls and a standing army?

Joshua, Israel's new leader, came face-to-face with God. Imagine the scene: Out surveying the layout of this new land of theirs near Jericho (their initial military obstacle), the first inhabitant Joshua encounters is a warrior.

This warrior had drawn His sword and pointed it into the sternum of Joshua.

Joshua asks this imposing figure; "Are you for us or against us?"

"Neither," He replies. "I am here to take over the coming

battle." The warrior describes himself as the Commander of the Lord's Hosts (armies). Joshua hits the deck, face down on the ground in reverence and asks, "What message does my Lord have for His servant?" As He had instructed Moses before him, this Commander of the Lord's armies replies, "Take off your sandals, for the place where you are standing is holy." And Joshua did so. (Most theologians believe this 'warrior' was the pre-incarnate Christ – Jesus, before He came to earth as a man, born of a woman.)

God instructs Joshua precisely how He wants Israel to conquer Jericho. They were to march Israel's army around the city once, led by the Ark of the Covenant and the priests blowing the ram's horns. They were to do so every day for six days. On the seventh day, they were to march around the city seven times, give a long blast on the horns, have the whole army yell and watch what God would do as the army marched straight into the city.

They did exactly as instructed. At the Big Yell, Jericho's "walls came a-tumblin' down" and the city fell completely. The army of Israel went straight into the city through the rubble with Rahab and her family being spared, its only survivors, as Joshua's spies had promised.

8. Judgment

At the end of the Israelite journey, of course, came physical death. For now I want you to realize this is not "the end" but in fact the beginning of our eternal existence, as it is for all mankind.

The Christian Journey

The journey of Israel is a well-documented and historical fact. I have even been to the Museum of Egyptian Antiquities in Cairo, seen and touched the very hieroglyphics that refer to Israel's exodus. But what does their journey have in common with today's Christians? As I read the accounts of Israel's deliverance out of bondage, lack of faith, and eventual trust in God's leading in their lives, I can't help but see the Christian journey, as well. The correlation is clear.

(See **Figure 2-2. Overview of the Christian Journey**.

The Christian's timeline:

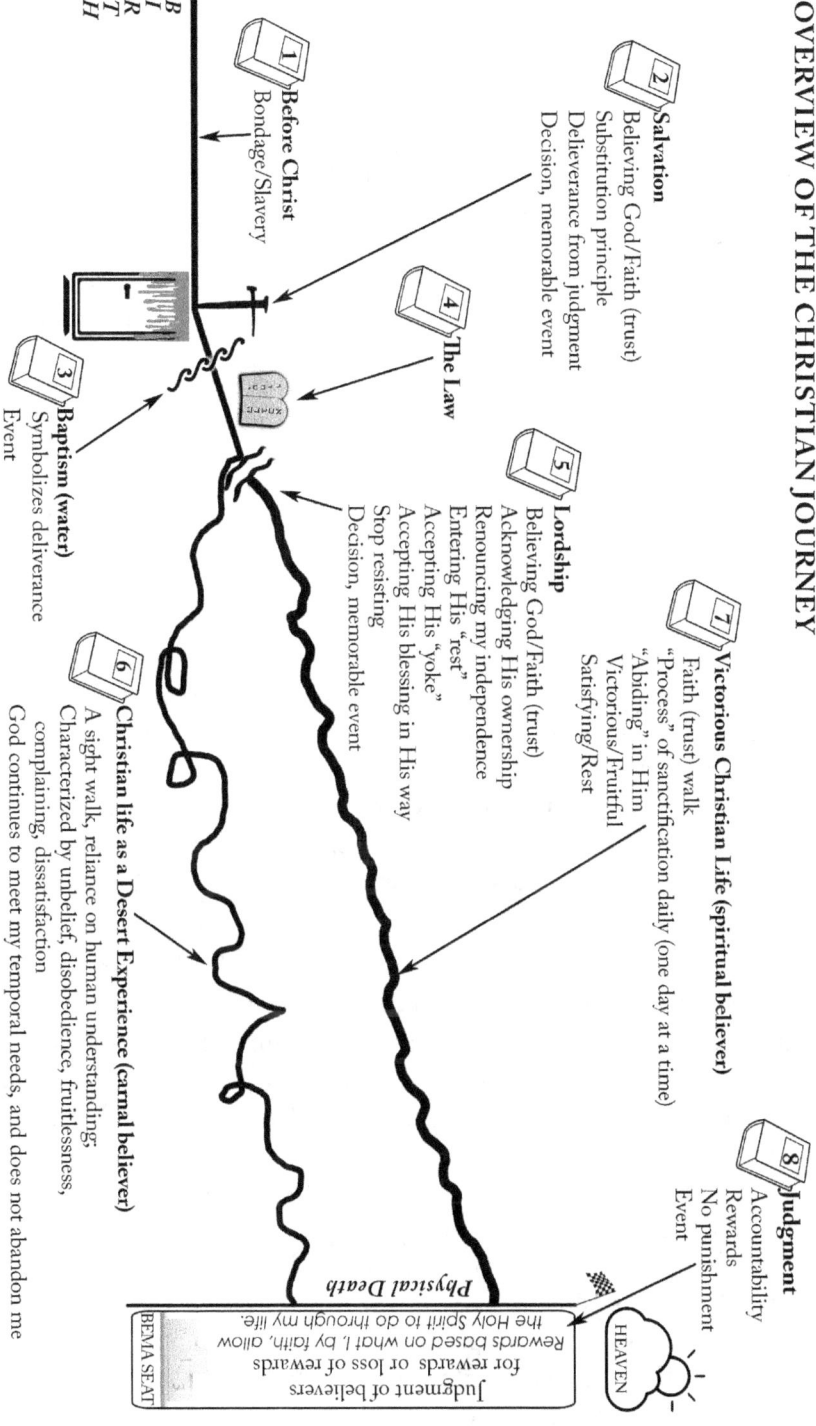

Figure 2-2

1. Before Christ: Bondage and Slavery to Sin

Just as the Israelites were in bondage before they were led out of Egypt, before we accepted Christ's atonement for our lives we too were trapped in bondage – the bondage of sin. We were slaves to our fallen nature, constantly choosing to do what was right in our own eyes. These sinful acts were not only acceptable but often pleasurable. The more we chose to go our own way, the better we thought of our decisions. The only time we found sin distasteful or unacceptable was when we were held accountable for it. Being held accountable by people, family and friends, society, or even God, is a very unpleasant experience. Like Adam and Eve, we attempt all types of deflection, blaming others, denial, covering up – all to avoid the consequences of our self-will. That avoidance practice is so well tuned and rooted in us there truly is no way to change our ways and we find ourselves in the chains of our bondage. It's there – in that place of dreaded realization – that God, the lover of our soul, graciously presents Himself through the person of Jesus Christ.

It's important to note that often we can't see our condition and our utter depravity. Some of us will spend much if not all of our lives trapped in the bondage of sin.

Some say, "I don't need God. He is just a crutch for the weak."

I simply observe, "If that's true, then, in whom do you trust?"

The answer is usually, "Honestly, the only one I can trust is myself."

As much as I might like to, I don't 'Dr. Phil' them with his famous semi-serious, pseudo-concerned sneer: "and how's that working out for ya?" This usually gets a big laugh from the audience, but also gets embarrassed silence from the person, shutting down any response. Instead, I will reply: "Help me understand … how does that work … honestly?"

Many say, "I choose what I want, what I will do, who I will depend on, and how I will live my life."

My response is always, "That may be true, but can you stop doing the things you choose?"

When you can't stop, my friend, you are in bondage.

So, I'll ask, again: "How are you doing?"

It's only when we are weak and that Christ's power may rest on us – and by His power, we are made strong.

2. A Deliverer Comes: Salvation

Just like the nation of Israel, we find ourselves in bondage. Israel was graciously given a deliverer, Moses. Christians also find themselves in bondage and, when we come to the end of our own resources and the end of our selves, there, right in the precise moment of need, God presents a deliverer, a spotless lamb. He delivers a substitution for those who will put their faith in Jesus' death, burial, and resurrection as payment for their sins. Then we are released from our bondage, saved from our sins, and re-made ("re-born") to live the life God had always intended for us!

Embracing the cross at Calvary and Jesus the Lamb of God who takes away the consequence of sin (death) for the world becomes the blood-painted doorpost of the Passover. Jesus' burial sets us free from the bondage of sin, and we are raised again as new creatures, literally new people free from the power of sin in our lives through the resurrection. This is simply lavish generosity on God's part.

We owe Him a debt for our sin and self-will. It is a debt we could never pay to justify ourselves in the face of God's justice. So, God takes it upon Himself to settle our accounts by sending His own – and *only* Son, to personally pay for something we can never repay ourselves! He doesn't stop there. He gives us a whole new life and sets us free from the bondage we are in.

That life, like His relationship with the Nation of Israel, is given to us with an abundance that we cannot possibly think or imagine! All He asks of us is to live out our new lives as generously as He gave them to us.

This is the God who, in Exodus 6:7, says to Israel: "I will take you as my own people, and I will be your God. Then you will know that I am the Lord your God, who brought you out from under the yoke of the Egyptians."

The same God, in John 15:9-10, says to you: "As the Father has loved me, so have I loved you. Now remain in my love. If you keep my commands, you will remain in my love, just as I have kept my Father's commands and remain in His love."

3. Baptism: First Water Experience

Just as with the Nation of Israel, Christ asks us to solidify our deliverance by willingly entering the water and being baptized. This signifies the death to life transformation that has already occurred through salvation. As with the parting of the Red Sea, we confirm to ourselves and to the world around us that we have been set free from the bondage of sin that we once lived in. By submersion into the water, the old life is left behind, and with immersion, the new life has come. Literally, the dead man is gone. We are made new again.

4. God's Law: His will becomes our desire

Israel was more than familiar with what God wanted for them. But God wanted (and wants) His desires to become our desires. So, God gave Israel the Ten Commandments, His perfect and Holy Law. The problem is that although the law can show him what sin is, man cannot fulfill it, nor really even desires to do so. Our bondage keeps us focused on our self-will.

But when this Generous God gives the Christian a new life in Christ, the law no longer is a rule to keep; but rather, a desire of our Father's that we willingly choose to do. It is no longer a set of rules (religion) that we are compelled to keep in order to please God. Now, because of God's generosity, His loving-kindness and patience, we want nothing more than to be more pleasing to Him. Do you see the difference?

Let me explain this from my own life. While I was still in bondage to my sinful selfishness, I gave little thought about sin or whether I was pleasing God. I liked sin. In fact, the more sin, the better. What I didn't like was the consequences of my sin such as how friends or family were disappointed and devalued when I lied. I never saw the *sin* as the problem – only how I was *treated* when I sinned. Then, in order to find relief from the consequences of my sinful selfishness, like Adam and Eve, I would go to great lengths to justify myself and relieve those consequences – NOT the sin – just the consequences.

When Jesus delivered me from bondage, and I became NEW, what a change! I became concerned with God's desires, not my own. Because I saw God's extraordinary generosity in my life, I wanted to do nothing but thank Him with a God-pleasing life. My desires changed and my affections were directed towards God. I wanted nothing more than to know this God and His Son, Jesus, who had been so generous to me. I remember thinking, 'What's wrong with me? I don't care about anything but Jesus!' The law became guardrails along my road in life. Like a real road, God's guardrails were for my safety in case of inattention or distraction. It was not my life's focus. Living my life in Christ was my focus. Carefully navigating each twist and turn of the road became my desire and my practiced skill. Could I punch through those guardrails? Sure I could, but I know that disaster is on the other side! As the Apostle Paul put it, the law became my schoolmaster to teach me God's desires for my life; living outside of God's Law is the antithesis of living in Christ. What must be understood is living outside of God's Law cheats us out of God's blessings!

5. Lordship (Ownership): The Second Water Experience

Over the years, as I have worked for some of the most prolific evangelists in the world, I have been involved in conversations regarding salvation, a person's commitment to Christ, the fruit or evidence of their being born again, and how to know if the evangelistic endeavor bears the fruit commensurate to the effort expended. The message of salvation is simple, radical and even offensive as well as foolishness to those who hear it. More importantly, the life of one who has surrendered his life to Christ can be a more powerful example of who Jesus is than all the preaching we can muster. I think everyone can agree that a life conformed in the likeness of Christ does offer the proof of the living God.

Why then do so many Christians live unholy, un-conformed, cheap, and hypocritical lives? Simply put, to lead a life conformed in the likeness of Christ, Jesus must be the owner of our lives. God has paid the highest price, His Son, for each of us. He bought us, He owns us, and now He wants to have access to every part of our lives. He now requires us to "get in the wheelbarrow and ride," renouncing our self-obsessed "independence" and acknowledging His ownership of our lives. Just as God led the Israelites to the Jordan River and instructed them to cross over into the Promised Land, He is asking you to trust Him with all of your life, all of your understanding, all of your relationships, all of your time, all of your possessions … EVERYTHING!

Some time ago, a man named John attended one of my conferences. I couldn't help but notice he wore a prosthetic leg. After getting to know him, I asked him how he lost his leg. The story he told was surprising and heart breaking – yet, what the Lord did with it and in him was simply amazing. John got caught up in the mortgage debacle of 2008. Ultimately, he was sentenced to prison. While incarcerated he was sent to a prison camp in Texas. The particular housing unit where he was assigned had a group shower – meaning each shower stall drained into a common drain in the middle of the room. This drain was partially obstructed and drained very slowly, causing water to back-up into the shower stalls. While working there, John had developed some nasty blisters on his feet from the cheaply-made boots provided by the prison system. The blisters and the filthy water turned into a potentially deadly combination. Despite John diligently working to keep his feet clean, in fresh socks, and changing the bandages on the blisters every day, they became infected from the bacteria-infested shower water.

John immediately sought medical attention for the infection.

It took weeks to actually see the doctor, which is, unfortunately, a common scenario in American (if not all) prison systems. While the doctor did prescribe oral antibiotics, sadly, the prison pharmacy took another two weeks to fulfill the prescription (again, a common medical reality that prison inmates encounter). By now John's infection was raging, affecting his overall health. He got feverish and began to get cold sweats.

Finally, one of the correctional officers (CO) noticed his difficulty walking and asked to see John's leg. John pulled up his pants to reveal a swollen and inflamed leg. The CO said, "I'll be right back." Within minutes, John was in a wheelchair and headed to the front gate of the prison to be checked out and taken to the local hospital. It's important at this point of the story to point out that this particular CO was extremely physically fit and a very large man. He also was a Christian. The lieutenant and a medical officer of the prison met them at the front gate. An argument pursued about this inmate being authorized to leave the camp, and whether this was a medical emergency and if it was a good use of prison financial resources. This argument ended when the CO said to his superiors, "You and six more like you will not stop me from taking this man to the hospital!" A few more threats were exchanged, including one to terminate the CO's employment. Nevertheless, the CO took John to the hospital.

Chapter 2: We Own Nothing

Upon arriving at the hospital's emergency room, John was discovered to have MRSA (Methicillin-resistant Staphylococcus aureus), a deadly staph infection that is so significant that every diagnosis must be reported to the Center for Disease Control and Prevention (CDC). MRSA cases are a common occurrence within the prison system. As John was being admitted, the CO inquired when he should return to retrieve John to return him to the prison camp. The admitting doctor replied, "It will be days, even weeks."

What came next sent a chill up the CO's spine. The doctor added, "I will not be surprised if this man doesn't lose his leg."

Days later, John lost his right leg, just below the knee.

By the time John related this story to me, it had been four years since his hospital stay. In that time, he had gone through weeks of recovery and rehabilitation and months of learning to walk again on his prosthetic leg. John's legal conviction and subsequent incarceration cost him many years of his life, his leg and much of his future. That day, when I had the honor of hearing his story, I asked; "How do you keep such a positive attitude with so much tragedy this has cost you?" His response astounded me.

"Mike, all that God has done for me, the price He paid, the price of His only Son on the cross, I recognize that He owns all of me. If He demands my years, my leg or my life — I gladly give it in return." Can you say the same? According to Scripture, we are NOT our own. We were bought at a price – the highest price – God's own Son.

> **"IF HE DEMANDS MY YEARS, MY LEG OR MY LIFE – I GLADLY GIVE IT."**

Ironically, one of the very prisons to which John was remanded has the following verse on an entrance placard: "Greater love has no one than this: to lay down one's life for one's friends. – John 15:13" This generous God of ours has demonstrated His great love for us by laying down His life for us. He simply asks us to do the same and trust Him with our lives, a life He already owns. The other man committed to Christ's ownership was the CO.

It occurs to me that you might be wondering what happened with the CO who bravely trusted God with his career and future, by violating a direct order and saving John's life. The CO returned to work and nothing good or bad was ever said. The word had gotten

HOW GOD BRINGS CHANGE

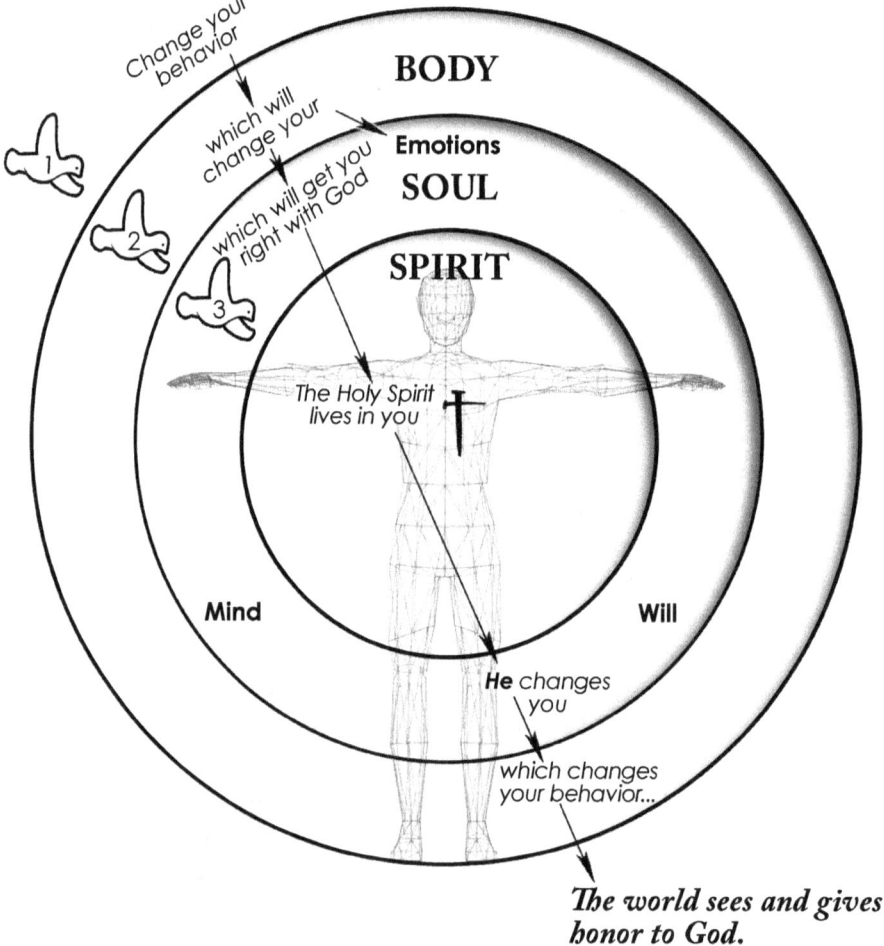

Figure 2-3

around about John losing his leg. Rather than following through with the threat of termination, the powers that be just remained silent. The CO continues to serve the Lord at the prison in his own way as Israel did. God only asks for our complete trust to cross over our Jordan River of ownership and into the life He has for us: A promised land of a life with no reservation.

6. Desert Living

Sadly, I believe that most Christians refuse to make that crossing. We think we know our lives better than He does and so we spend our lives usurping God's ownership of our lives. We'll allow God access to some of the areas of our lives, but not all. Like disobedient children, we spend our days negotiating with God over things we willfully want to do, possess, or believe. We sense that the Holy Spirit is a gentleman and is asking us to trust Him. He wants to change some things about our understanding, our behavior, and how we see our possessions. But, we are reluctant to change our minds about some of those areas as we become challenged about them. What is interesting is that He only wants to work on areas based on His priorities for our lives, as He brings understanding that's appropriate for our spiritual maturity.

Let me explain. (Please see **Figure 2-3. How God Brings Change** on the facing page.)

Man is a three part being.

We have a **spirit**: which is our deep, personal, unshakable, non-intellectual and non-emotional, reality-based awareness of God – our "*God*-awareness." It is one of the things that makes us unique in all of God's creation. Apart from God's salvation, our own spirit lacks life. Once we accept God's atoning sacrifice of His Son, the Holy Spirit takes up residence in us, bringing our spirit alive.

We have a **soul**: our *self*-awareness. Because God has created us with a soul, we know we exist. We know we are individuals. The soul is where our mind, will, and emotions reside. Upon salvation, our mind needs to be changed. Our will needs to be conformed. Our emotions need control. All of which is now possible because the Holy Spirit now resides in us.

We have a **body**: our world awareness. Our body is the outward shell we all see. It's corruptible and is slowly dying. Because we have a body, we can interact with the world around us. This body is certainly corruptible, *i.e.*, susceptible to physical harm, disease, and death. Through our body, we demonstrate behavior with which the world around us interacts. When we pass from this life, the only part of us we leave behind (besides others' memories of us) is our corruptible body. In Heaven, we get a new body, which is perfect and non-corruptible.

It is through His created system of the three-part "us," that God works to conform us to the image of Christ. He desires to change us from the inside out. Now that He has taken residence in our lives, The Holy Spirit wants to make changes to our mind, our will, and our emotions. As He makes those changes our behavior begins to change. Our "internals" dictate our "externals" and our new inner attitudes direct a new outer behavior and interaction with the world around us. It's important to see that God makes these changes to glorify Himself through us. As those changes become observable, the world around us sees the changes in our lives and gives honor to God.

It's important to note that this system, created by God, is in direct opposition to the world's system which was invented by man on his own so that he could retain for himself control over his own life.

Every non-Christian religion, self-improvement theory or recovery program theoretically works like this: First, you change your behavior. Next, maintain that new behavior. Then, when you've maintained that new behavior long enough, your mind, your will, and your emotions will change. Their belief is, if you *act better*, you *become better* — your "externals" drive your "internals." For the non-Christian religious, this promises that if you continue that new "better" behavior, as your soul changes, you will become more acceptable to God.

The problem is that it doesn't work like that, because that is a lie. Fad diets come and go, addicts use again, criminals re-offend and the relationally-challenged leave a growing string of devastated people in their wake. It becomes a religion unto itself this constantly trying to become acceptable to God by our own acts and trying to do something that was already done (and could only really be done) for us by Jesus.

God wants to effect His changes in your life. But when you don't accept God's ownership over your life, He won't make the changes

He desires until you give Him that authority by fully trusting Him. This hesitation results in the average Christian living a mediocre life – "wandering in the (spiritual) desert." Like Israel, many Christians live their lives in this desert. Their lives are filled with fruitlessness, dissatisfaction, and complaining. They have a "sight walk" represented by simply following the pillar of fire by night and cloud by day, as Israel did – not the walk of faith and the trust of a life-surrendered Christian. Because they belong to God, He provides for them, just as He provided for Israel through manna, meat, water and clothing. However, these desert-living Christians are never satisfied with God's provision and always want more. Real spiritual battles don't seem to happen in their lives, just a dissatisfaction within. Because they have no battles, they have no victories. They seldom celebrate their lives as Christians. Instead they wander aimlessly through life just waiting for it to end through death or the rapture.

7. Living in the Promised Land

God wants so much more for your life than a form of religion that isn't fulfilling. What a contrast! God has created us new again so we can have the generous life that He set for us before the beginning of time - a life that exceeds our imagination.

Now I don't know about you, but I can imagine a lot! Now, I don't mean money and possessions, though those may be tools He gives to us in this world to glorify Him and fulfill His desires. I mean a deeply satisfying life, rich full relationships, and an opportunity to invest in eternity. This life in Christ is full of joy and contentment regardless of your circumstances.

The Apostle Paul put it this way:

> ... I have learned to be content whatever the circumstances. I know what it is to be in need, and I know what it is to have plenty. I have learned the secret of being content in any and every situation, whether well fed or hungry, whether living in plenty or in want. I can do all this through Him who gives me strength.
> Philippians 4:11b-13 (NIV)

As with Israel, God has called every Christian into a walk of faith, trusting in Him. He promises that for this life in Christ, He will provide all that you need – and beyond. He promises that as you live this life of dependence upon Him, He will personally give you the victory in all of the battles you encounter, and – as you trust in Him – victories, in His time and in His way.

As you have seen with Israel, He had already conquered the hearts of the inhabitants of Jericho for His people. But, He also went to battle for them, personally giving them instructions that would seem crazy to most people. Yelling, marching, and blowing horns doesn't seem like a battle plan from man's standpoint. But when they trusted God and followed His plan in this place of trust, all was provided—well beyond all they could want or imagine.

Christian, this analogy begs just one question: Where are you? Are you a desert-living Christian, walking aimlessly through your spiritual life? Is your life full of dissatisfaction, complaints, and fruitlessness? Are you lacking the spiritual battles that bring the heavenly victories you long for? Do you compartmentalize your faith from the rest of your life? Do you justify yourself with thoughts like: "what I do at work is my business and church is church?" Or, "I know I shouldn't look at or read those things, but I deserve some time off from religion." Or, my personal favorite, "I've done enough God stuff this week already." If any of these statements remotely sounds like you, then the Holy Spirit, who is living in you, will not change your mind, your will, or your emotions in order to conform you into the image of Christ. That's why your life is so unfulfilling!

> **"CHRISTIAN – WHERE ARE YOU?"**

On the other hand, if you identify as one who has fully surrendered to allowing the Holy Spirit access to every part of your understanding, possessions, and your physical life; and if you are satisfied with your life in Christ, regardless of your circumstances; and if you are more than willing to allow the Holy Spirit access to your mind, your will, and your emotions, then know this: He always wants His best in your life. Your goal is to be conformed to the image of the One who saved you, with your character looking more and more like Jesus every day. Not because "you" are making those changes; but instead, it's a work of the Holy Spirit in you. As this happens, you will likely want to declare from the rooftops "Jesus is my Lord! He owns me and I am willing to give Him all!"

8. Judgment

For the Christian comes another judgment upon physical death. It's a judgment of accountability but not punishment. This will be explained in further detail in Chapter 6.

For now I want you to consider your life today. Are you walking in the Promised Land or, like so many, are you a desert-living Christian?

Christian, if you find yourself living in the desert there is good news. You don't need to stay there! Acknowledge that He owns you and you have been usurping His authority in your life. Do it through prayer.

Pray something like this:

> "Jesus, I certainly don't know what You have planned for my life, and to be honest I have some fears, but I do understand that You own me. I cannot possibly make the best decisions for life, since I don't know what You want to make of me, nor what is involved in that process. I am thankful that You do know and I want to trust You alone to make the appropriate changes. Thank You for letting me be part of Your plans."

WELCOME
to a
Life Without Reservation!

Chapter 3
WHOSE ARE YOU?

On September 17, 1862, as the sun set on the bloodiest day of the Civil War, 6,000 Americans lay dead on the field of Antietam.[1] Another 17,000 were wounded,[2] more than four times the American death toll of D-Day during World War ll. God had answered President Lincoln's desperate prayer for victory at Antietam, and General Lee retreated from Pennsylvania back to Virginia. President Lincoln had made a prayerful promise to God: "I made a solemn vow before God, that if General Lee was driven back from Pennsylvania, I would crown the result by declaration of freedom to the slaves."[3] True to his word, our sixteenth President of the United States did what he promised to God.

On September 22, 1862, The Emancipation Proclamation was issued, which stated the Negro slave deserved to live as free people do. However, the combination of the perception that this would cause the war to linger and the negative reaction to the proclamation resulted in political strife our country had never seen before or since. In the House of Representatives, Ohio Congressman Clement Vallandigham spoke words that some considered treason: "Ought this war continue? No – not a day, nor an hour!"[4] The war that had been initiated to save the Union was now a war for the Negro.[5] Vallandigham called for the soldiers to go home, adding that if the North didn't want a peaceful nation with slavery intact, let them form their own nation.[6] Delaware Senator Willard Saulsbury Sr. called Lincoln an "Imbecile" and "the weakest man ever placed in high office."[7] When the senator was called to order, he refused to yield the floor and the sergeant at arms was called to remove him. The senator then pulled a gun and threatened to shoot the sergeant at arms.[8]

---

1 National History Education Clearing House https://teachinghistory.org/history-content/ask-a-historian/24265
2 *Ibid.*
3 Wellman's Miscellany, Volumes 5-7; Page 113
4 Abraham Lincoln: A Biography - Page 379
5 Copperhead Politics; https://en.wikipedia.org/wiki/Copperhead_(politics)
6 *Ibid.*
7 Revolvy; https://www.revolvy.com/page/Willard-Saulsbury-Sr.
8 *Ibid.*

And we think today's political climate is difficult!

This political turmoil, along with the continued heavy losses in the war, contributed to nearly breaking the resolve of the North. The Rebel Confederacy's General Robert E. Lee and its President Jefferson Davis were convinced one more victory for the South would end the war. As both armies settled in at Gettysburg, Pennsylvania, the South was convinced it would easily take Washington, D.C. The Government and residents knew of their impending peril. "Something of a panic pervades the city," recorded Secretary of the Navy, Gideon Welles.[9] Thousands were set to flee before General Lee's army arrived. Some of Lincoln's cabinet urged him to leave Washington: "You cannot wait here for Lee's army to capture the city. You cannot humiliate yourself, our army, or the union by remaining here. Think of the repercussions if you are captured! If you want to keep fighting, you are going to have to go!"[10]

Lincoln went into his private office and fell to his knees in prayer, later journaling:

> *Never before had I prayed with so much earnestness. I wish I could repeat my prayer. I felt I must put all my trust in Almighty God. He gave our people the best country ever given to man. He alone could save it from destruction. I had tried my best to do my duty and I found myself unequal to the task. The burden was more than I could bear. I asked Him to help us and give victory now: I was sure my prayer was answered. I had no misgiving about the result at Gettysburg.*[11]

Over the three-day battle of Gettysburg, a constant stream of conflicting reports came into the White House. No one seemed to know either what was really going on, or who was winning. But, even as President Lincoln's army could be facing a devastating defeat, he

---

9 Diary of Gideon Wells https://archive.org/stream/diaryofgideonwel00well/diaryofgideonwel00well_djvu.txt
10 General Dan Sickles: http://www.mrlincolnswhitehouse.org/residents-visitors/marys-charlatans/marys-charlatans-general-dan-sickles-1819-1914/
11 *Ibid.*

was described as being in excellent spirits.[12] General James Rusling gave this account of Lincoln's response upon asking Lincoln about his calmness:

> *Well, I'll tell you how it was. In the pinnacle of the campaign up there, when everyone seems panic-stricken, and nobody could tell what was going to happen, oppressed by the gravity of our affairs, I went to my room one day and locked the door and got down on my knees before Almighty God, and prayed to Him that this was His war, and our cause His cause; but, we couldn't stand another Fredericksburg or Chancellorsville ... soon a sweet comfort crept into my soul that God Almighty had taken the whole business into His own Hands and that things would go alright in Gettysburg.*[13]

Casualties at Gettysburg totaled 23,049 for the Union (3,155 dead, 14,529 wounded, 5,365 missing) compared to the Confederate casualties at 28,063 (3,903 dead, 18,735 injured, and 5,425 missing).[14] But the North did win, and the South's defeat was colossal. For the South, their hope for a European intervention ended and what followed was a series of battles lost to the North. Two years later, on April 9, 1865, facing starvation and increasing ruin, General Robert E. Lee surrendered at Appomattox ending the most bloody and brutal episode in United States history. Estimates are that 640,000-700,000 soldiers died saving the union and ending slavery. The United States was reunited, slavery outlawed, and democracy preserved for the nation.

Without battles, there are no victories.

What is important to note is that with the Emancipation Proclamation, and ultimately, with the passage of the 13th Amendment to the Constitution, the American slaves were free – totally, legally,

---
12 General Dan Sickles: http://www.mrlincolnswhitehouse.org/residents-visitors/marys-charlatans/marys-charlatans-general-dan-sickles-1819-1914/
13 The Souls of Abraham Lincoln; out of print: https://archive.org/stream/.../soulabrahamlinc02bartgoog_djvu.txt
14 HistoryNet: www.historynet.com/battle-of-gettysburg

Life Without Reservation

and in every way, as by its two sections:

> Neither slavery nor involuntary servitude, except as a punishment for crime whereof the party shall have been duly convicted, shall exist within the United States, or any place subject to their jurisdiction.
>
> *– and –*
>
> Congress shall have power to enforce this article by appropriate legislation.
> – Amendment XIII to the Constitution of the United States of America, (complete text)

So, what was the response of the massive slave population in the United States?

Nothing.

There were no celebrations and no dancing in the streets. In fact, the next day, most slaves returned back to the fields they worked before being freed.

Many anthropologists say it was because they were uneducated, denied the information proclaiming their freedom, that they were lied to by their slave owners, or just knew no other life and had nowhere to go.[15] I believe all of these were probably true.

Imagine if:
- You had spent your life being dehumanized and denied education, so you couldn't read a newspaper or hear the news of your freedom.
- You knew no other life or place to live because you'd spent your life on the few acres you worked, only experiencing life outside the plantation for brief hours at a time, if at all.
- The only authority you ever knew was your owner and his deputies, who often ruled harshly with little regard to your value, other than the work you provided?

---
15 PBS; https://www.pbs.org/wgbh/aia/part4/4p2956.html

- You were raised from birth as a beast of burden, your only purpose being to work so your master could prosper.

It's a life far from what I have ever lived. But I do have a bit of an idea of it. If you have read my biography, you have learned the many things God has accomplished in my life, including spending some years in prison and many years outside prison serving and ministering to inmates and their families.

There is much I could write about God and His faithfulness to the millions of inmates incarcerated around the world, but for now, I want to share just one concept of God's internal work in man. A concept that a modern-day prisoner may be uniquely positioned to understand – a position perhaps similar to where the American slaves were back in that moment in history.

When a person is locked-up and their freedom is taken away, there begins a deliberate process of dehumanizing the prisoner. You are chained hand and foot. Completely stripped of all your clothing, every body cavity is explored while you're verbally and sometimes physically humiliated. All hints of your personal identity – such as your clothes, your jewelry, and your name – are taken from you. You and every other prisoner are dressed in identical, cheap, and often worthless clothes. The government, the media, prison officials, friends, family, and society berate you. No matter what your life or status was on the "outside," no matter your past affluence or influence, you lose all of that. In everyone's eyes (soon to include your eyes, too) you become less than human, now that you are on the "inside." No matter what your education was – or what your IQ is, you are treated as stupid and worthless, having NO valuable input or thought to improve your environment or your situation in life. Your food is decided and even provided for you at the whim of the officer serving it. Often, it's beyond expiration, spoiled, or even full of insects. A warm meal – *i.e.*, one that is *supposed* to be warm – is a luxury and the posted menu is actually a public relations piece to keep elected officials and other "concerned parties" satisfied. Medical care is sub-standard, and often, serious illnesses go untreated for years – until severe damage (or death) demands attention (remember my friend, John, the amputee from Chapter 2? His "medical care" was atypical.). Minor infractions are treated with the harshest of penalties. Even when the President of the United States issues an Executive Order to cease any such inappropriately harsh practice,[16] it is ignored and the harsh punishments simply continue – just as inappropriately harsh, as before.

Rules and procedures are, as well, at the whim of whoever is in charge at the moment. They are often applied capriciously and abusively. Vital information is purposely kept from you. Mis- (or no) information is the rule. Contact with the "outside" is limited and actually discouraged in both practice and policy. Prisoners are often forced to work for the benefit of the State, providing a valuable workforce of menial and intellectual labor, to benefit the people they work for, so *they* can prosper.

In very similar ways, a prisoner lives the life of a slave, forced into a dehumanized state, one that strips all value from living. And just as the slaves did at their Emancipation, when a prisoner returns to freedom (to which 99% will), they, too, mostly return to exactly the same life they always knew – although now, their life-image and self-worth has been taken from them. There are no celebrations, no dancing. Just fear.

Why do I align these parallels together in a book about living a life without reservation?

Because this is the Good News, the Gospel, that Jesus brought to us all:

We have a Deliverer, One Who set the captives free! (Luke 4:18-21)

But, not only did He free us – like a "freed" slave or prisoner – He made us NEW (Col 2:13; 3:10; Eph 2:24; and Gal 6:14-15) by giving us a new identity. (Rev 2: 17; 2Cor 5:17; and Gal 6:14-15) He did it all couched in empathy. (Heb 2:18 and 4:15-16) Empathy that only comes by living the experience Himself. (Phil 2:8 and John 1:12-14) Jesus emptied His Godself, taking the form of man, even though He was fully God. (Phil 2:5-7 and Col 1:15-20) Fully God – born fully man, He humbled Himself – becoming obedient; and completely submissive to His Heavenly Father's will in living out His devalued (*i.e.*, fully-human versus divine) state, even to the point of death on a cross, the most humiliating death of its time. (Phil 2:8; Gal 3:13; and Deut 21:23) He was Isaiah's prophesied Messiah for God's chosen people – but, He found, taught, and led them as a teacher-servant. Why? So He could work and will His life within

---

16 Obama White House: https://obamawhitehouse.archives.gov/the-press-office/2016/01/25/fact-sheet-department-justice-review-solitary-confinement

us for His good pleasure.

Christian, Jesus lived His earthly life so we could be completely free from the power, pollution, and consequences of this life and be made new and complete in Him, (Col 1:15-20 and 2:9-10) as an adopted child of God the Father. (John 1:12)

> **"JESUS LIVED HIS EARTHLY LIFE SO WE COULD BE COMPLETELY FREE FROM THE POWER, POLLUTION, AND CONSEQUENCES OF THIS LIFE AND BE MADE NEW AND COMPLETE IN HIM."**

Imagine how the American slave would have responded if (for example), on the day he was set free, the master would have taken the slave out of his dismal living conditions, brought him into the mansion, washed him clean, dressed him in the finest of clothes, fed him, and officially, legally, adopted him as his son, by giving this once-slave his name and the full rights to all he owned. Then the master threw a party the likes of which no one has ever or would ever see again.

Now, imagine that former slave becoming fully aware that there was a great battle in which his master's own son had died. And the son died purposely so that the former slave could become the master's adopted son, with all the rights the natural son had. What joy, what celebration, what humility there would be in the heart of this once-enslaved-now-adopted son! Think of what the newly adopted son would need to learn to become a useful son and steward of his new father's name and estate.

My fellow Christian, this is what God, through His Son, Jesus, has done for you. (2 Cor 5:17-19) At the moment you trusted Christ, wonderful things happened to you (listed here in no particular order):

- All your sins were forgiven – past, present, and future – and the indebtedness those sins created was fully paid on your behalf. (Col 2:13-14)
- You became a child of God. (John 1:12; Rom 3:20-28; and John 5:24)
- You received eternal life with God. (John 1:12; Rom 3:20-28; and John 5:24)
- You were delivered from Satan's domain, into the

- Kingdom of Christ. (Col 1:13)
- You were declared righteous by God. (2 Cor 5:17)
- You entered into a love relationship (covenant) with God. (1 John 4:9-11)
- You became totally accepted by God. (Col 1:19-22)

A new life in Christ requires so complete a re-making of your nature and your relationship to God, it is referred to as a "new birth" – or "rebirth" – or even being "born again" in order to enter into that new life. (1 Pet 2:2 and John 3:3) You must be "reborn" into that new life – and that new life brings with it a new identity. (2 Cor 5:17)

It's not just a matter of "getting eternal life," rather it's about being someone new in a new relationship with God. Make no mistake; there are no other alternatives: *everyone* gets eternal existence after death – some spend it with God while others spend it … ah, well, … to be blunt: … in the 'smoking section.'

> "IT'S NOT JUST A MATTER OF "GETTING ETERNAL LIFE" UPON EARTH, RATHER IT'S ABOUT BEING SOMEONE NEW IN A NEW RELATIONSHIP WITH GOD."

When you were born again, you were transformed from the state you were physically *born* into (a sinner able to choose only to sin, *i.e.,* to rebel against God, and unable to do anything on your own to pay for the debt your sin creates)—into the state which God had in mind for you when He *created* you (a righteous person who could choose to obey God) and whom He loved so much, that He paid for all of your sins with the death of His only begotten Son.

Then, like the slave or the prisoner, you were not only transformed, but, adopted into the family of God, as well. You are now a child of the living God, with a new nature and a new relationship to your Father. He has adopted you, (John 1:12) giving you full rights as a son or daughter. With new life comes a new title and a new responsibility. In the New Testament, one of the most commonly used words for ordinary Christians is "saints" (1 Cor 1:2 and Rom 1:7) or 'holy people.' This is not a title we earn; but rather, one bestowed upon us by

God. We are related to God by Spiritual birth and nothing can change that blood (covenant) relationship. (John 10:27, 28; and Rom 8:35-39)

I am born again because of a Spiritual union with Him through His grace, which I received through my faith in the Good News of the scripture that I heard and—as the Holy Spirit made me able to do – believed. My relationship with God is forever settled. I am His son. (Gal 4:1-7) No one can change that, not even me. I did nothing to earn it, and I can do nothing to un-earn it. It was a TOTAL work of God through His Son, Jesus. (Eph 2:8-9)

It's true that at times I can disrupt my harmony with God, (2 Cor 6:14 and 1 John 1:6) and just like a natural child, I can be disobedient to my parents, resulting in disharmony in my relationship with them. However, NOTHING I can do will change my status as His child, (Rom 8:37-39) although, I will feel miserable as a result of the disharmony my disobedience would cause. My relationship with God is not in jeopardy, because I am related to Him through Christ's death, burial, and resurrection (Rom 8:28-38) and not because of any effort of my own. My acceptance, significance, and security are fully restored. These were lost in the Garden of Eden because of the fall of Adam. (1 Cor 15:22ff) But they are now restored through this new-birth-blood-relationship with Jesus (the second Adam). (1 Cor 15:45) Because of this completely new creation that I have become, (Psa 23:3 and Joel 2:25) the Bible says that now I am totally accepted because I am: God's child, Christ's friend, (John 1:12) totally justified, (Rom 3:24) united with the Lord, (Gal 3:28) bought with a price, (1 Cor 6:20) a member of Christ's body, (1 Cor 6:15) a saint, (1 Cor 1:1-3) adopted as God's own, (Rom 8:15) having full access to God, (Eph 2:18 and 3:12) fully redeemed and fully forgiven, (Col 2:13) and I am complete in Jesus Christ. (Col 2:10)

> The Bible also addresses my significance in Christ:
> - I am called salt and light for the world. (Matt 5:13-16)
> - I am a channel of His life, I bear His fruit. (Josh 1 and Gal 5)
> - I am His personal witness, (Acts 1:8) His temple, (1 Cor 6:19) His minister of reconciliation, (2 Cor 5:18-31 and 1 John 4:9-11), and His co-worker. (1 Cor 3:9)
> - I am seated with Him and have the freedom and

confidence to approach Him at any time. (Eph 2:6)
- I can do all things through Christ. (Phil 4:13)

I also find that the work of Christ has restored my security:
- I am assured all things work together for the good, (Rom 8:28)
- I am free from condemnation (Rom 8:1-2) and free of all charges against me. (Rom 8:33)
  » I am hidden in Christ, (Col 3:3) and I cannot be separated from God's love, (Rom 8:35-39)
  » I know that He will finish the work He began in me. (1 Thes 5:23)
  » I am a citizen of heaven, (Phil 3:20) I am free from fear, (Matt 10:26 and Luke 12:4) and I have all the mercy and grace I need. (Psa 23:6; Matt 6:30; and Eph 2:4-5, 8:45)
  » I am born of God! (John 1:12-13)

This complete work was done so we can now live the life without reservation that God intended for us when He created us and intends for us now that we have responded to His free offer of salvation through Jesus Christ. (Rom 8:28-30)

A life that is willfully submitted to God.
  A life empowered by God Himself. (Rom 6:3-8)
    A life that is free from slavery and fear. (Rom 6:6-7)
      A life that is confident in Whose I am, and
        A life that is confident in who God is. (2 Thes 3:3-6)

The problem lies in the fact that we have a difficult time believing these truths. Like the slave or prisoner, our minds need renewing (Rom 12:1-2) from the belief system of the "old self." (Rom 6:6-7) All too often, we return to the only lives we've known, (Heb 10:39) back to the same past life, – those same few acres of land, the same belief system and the same fear we had before God recreated us new.

> **"... WE HAVE A DIFFICULT TIME BELIEVING THESE TRUTHS."**

Look at **Figure 3-1. A New Believer Needs to Understand Human Nature**. (See next page.)

Our thinking is like a whiteboard at physical birth, a clean slate that begins to be written upon by the world, the flesh, and the devil. (1 John 2:15-17) But, as we are born into sin, (Psa 51:5) we do not 'fear the Lord' – we are not able to choose His ways for us on our own. (Psa 25:12)

Before knowing Christ, we go through a learning process from our parents, friends, television, education system, *etc.*, that forms an incomplete worldview. Before knowing Christ, we are predisposed towards self-reliance: independence from God, and reliance upon the works of our own behavior and doing. This becomes our own understanding – of reality and how it is structured, of how we fit into it, how to relate to others, and even how to relate to and use the items we possess. We are slaves to the sinful nature and dead in relationship to God. (Rom 6:19-23)

However, once Christ frees us from the power of the sinful nature into which we were born, we often don't understand the unchanged tendencies of our "old nature." Even as believers, we can have the same problem that the Galatian Christians had – trusting in their own goodness and works. (Gal 3:13) This is because the understanding and worldview we grew into before we were saved doesn't change at salvation, so, unexamined and unchallenged, we carry that whiteboard and all its accumulated written data into our new life in Christ.

Yet, as we allow the Holy Spirit to change our mind, our will, and our emotions using His Word (2 Tim 3:14-17 and Heb 4:11-13) and the application of His Word by faith, (James 2:22 and 1 John 5:4) little by little, He will illuminate the understanding and worldview that He wants to alter in us. He basically rewrites our mind, our will, and our emotions into having the mind of Christ, (Phil 2:5) and, all of this is rooted in the new, 'transformed,' (Rom 12:2) identity of who we are in Christ.

Often, our unchanged tendencies are based on seeking acceptance, significance, and security through a world-system viewpoint that cannot achieve any of these things for us with any real

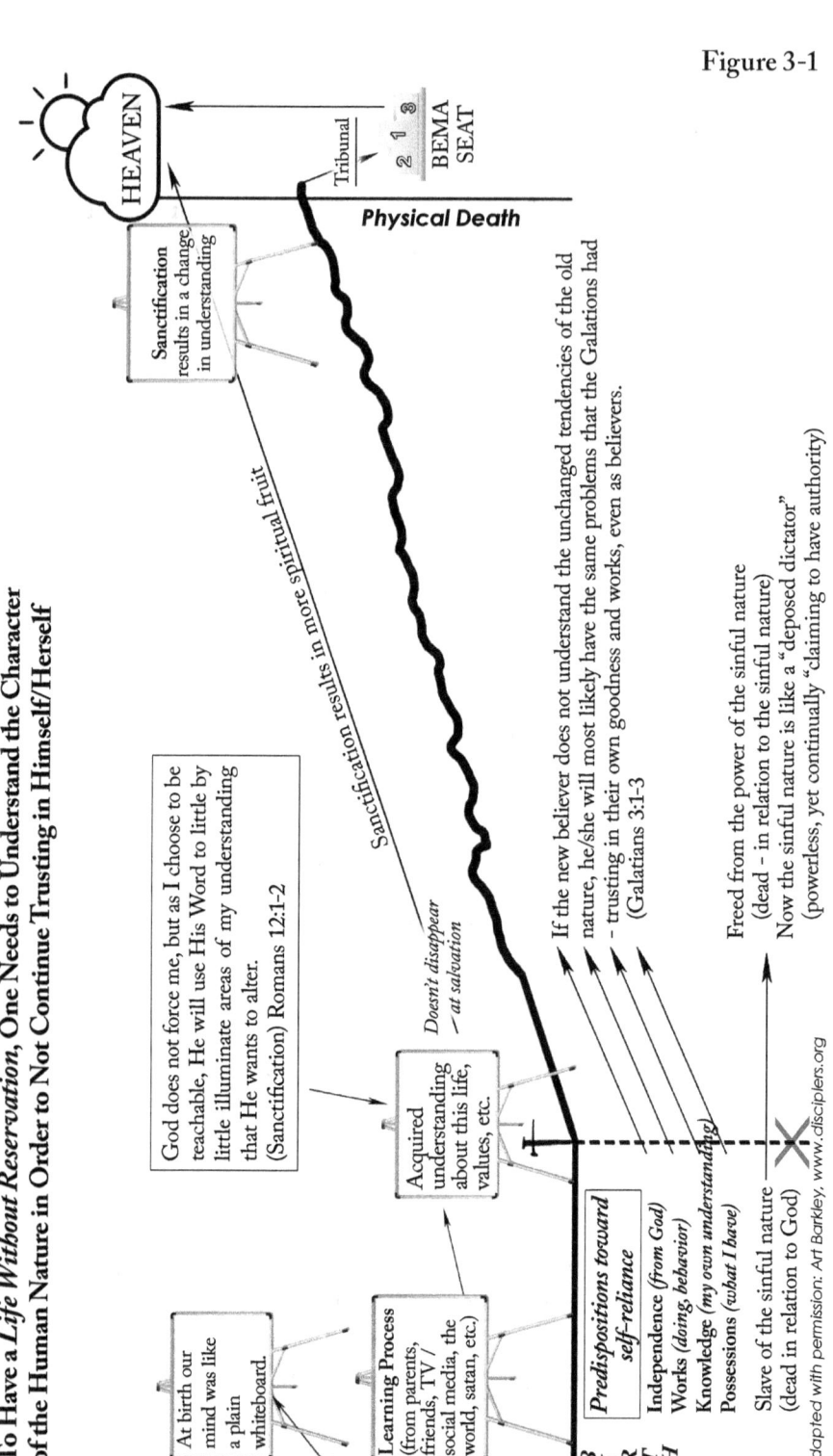

Figure 3-1

meaning. Our thinking becomes futile and our worldview becomes a house built on sand, looking as if it has substance, but easily undermined by the storms of life. (Luke 6:46-49) We are told by the world that we have no value, or that our value is based on performance, or what others think of us. We are so often lied to, so that the liar is lifted up and we are pushed down. Just like the American slaves after their emancipation, we don't leave behind the subjugation from which we have been freed.

This evil use of misinformation is designed to keep you from appropriating the victory Christ has already given you. Its accompanying fear keeps you from embracing your new life without reservation. This well-orchestrated battle for your mind begins with polarization: trying to separate you from God, then demonizing Him in your eyes, making God a tyrant so you question His motives. (Rom 12:2) Next, it's organization: The world system builds a nefarious campaign against God and His people for you (Rev 18:23) Finally, comes covert guile: relying on deceit and cunning, all the while using camouflage, (Mark 4:19 and 1 John 2:11) Satan lures you into thinking you are self-justified (2 John7; 1 Cor 6:9) when actually, you are self-deceived. (1 John 1:8; Gal 6:1-7; and James 1:22-26) You begin to trust your unchanged tendencies over what God says about you as well as Who and/Whose you are. (1 Cor 6:19-20) This is not a pretty picture!

Why all the effort?

Now that the world, the flesh, and the devil have lost you for eternity, the enemy's strategy is to keep you believing here on earth that you are NOT who God says you are. He wants you to live an ineffective Christian life filled with dissatisfaction and complaining, (1 Pet 5:8 and Rev 12:9) so that God will not get the glory of your life lived without reservation, and the world will not be able to see you living your life surrendered unto Him and give God the glory for it as you should be living it.

Why does it matter what God says about you? Why does it matter about *Who* He is and *Whose* you are?

YES! It matters because your belief about yourself determines your behavior. (Luke 6:40) Your behavior is a witness to God's faithfulness to mankind.

Simply put,

Do people deceive you?
(1 John 3:7 and 2 Pet 2:13)

    Does the world system deceive you?
    (2 Thes 2:3; Eph 5:6; and Eph 4:14)

        Does the devil deceive you?
        (1 John 2:11; Eph 6:12; and 1 Pet 5:8)

            Do you from time to time _deceive yourself_?
            (Gal 6:1-7; James 1:22-26; and 1 John 1:8)

Sure, they (and you) do.

So, who are you going to believe?

        What others (and you) say about you
                – or –
            what God says about you?

You, my friend, are a blood-bought child of a generous God! (1 Cor 6:19-20)

Now, move forward in life with the knowledge of *Who* God is and *Whose* you are.

Chapter 4
WHAT IS GENEROSITY?

When most people think about generosity, they think about money, philanthropy, fancy banquets, or giant checks given to charities on TV or in the newspaper. But, we are beginning to see that *Biblical* generosity is much more than that.

As I have discussed so far, we serve a generous God because generosity is part of His nature. Out of His very generous nature, He has given us ***everything***: light and life, mercy and grace, salvation and freedom, deliverance and a new identity in Him. (Col 1:1-14; Pet 1:1-9) He has even restored us to a full and complete relationship with Himself and all of His creation. (Rom 8; Eph Ch1-2)

Experiencing God's abundant generosity in our own lives, what can we be – but grateful? How can we live – but generously, both out of our gratitude for what He has done in our own lives *and* as He commands? Be assured, if God commands, or even just asks us to do something, He enables us to do that thing.

This Spiritual Gift of Generosity is a way of living in response to the generosity of God. It is a life returned unto God (2 Cor 9:6-15) with no expectation of earthly gain, no expectation of gratitude, or recognition, or return, either in-kind or in a greater amount. There's no expectation how the gift will be used or expended. It's given without the smallest of strings attached. Nor will there be a follow-up, to see if "good stewardship" was applied.

> "IT IS A LIFE RETURNED UNTO GOD..."

That's not to say that these things should not happen. It is simply to say that a life given freely has no transactional quality to it. That is, once it's given as a gift, it has been transferred to another, and its stewardship now becomes the responsibility of the receiving party. (Matt 25:31-46)

Let me illustrate: Years ago, I was a young leader of a homeless mission. One of the staff members was in need of a car. As a non-profit organization, our homeless mission was often given vehicles as donations, some running, some not. Some were decent, roadworthy, and very usable. Some were disposed of for parts. When I became aware of this staff member's need, the mission had an old, but roadworthy car on hand that had a few thousand miles left in her. So, at the next regular board of directors meeting, I proposed to the board that we give this car to the staff member in need. After a short discussion and prayer, it was unanimously agreed to transfer the title of the vehicle to the staff member to meet his need. This entire process took weeks, and, in that time, a local church had separately heard of this employee's need. Moving much faster than we could, they provided a much newer and better car. When I notified the staff member about our gift, he promptly advised me about the newer car, but asked if it would be alright if he could sell the older car the mission had gifted him and use the proceeds for insurance and a set of new tires. My answer, "we gave you this car as directed by the Holy Spirit. We prayed about it and unanimously decided that this is what God wanted to do. It's your car to do what you will with it before the Lord. We gave it as unto God." (Col 3:17-23) Sounds good, doesn't it?

At the next board meeting, I mentioned in passing the disposition of our "gift." What happened next, I didn't foresee. The board was completely – to a person – offended that he sold the car. The more they talked about it, the angrier they got. One member yelled, "We didn't give him that car to sell! We could have used the money to help the homeless!" My response; "Didn't we all agree to give it to him? Didn't we all pray together? Didn't we decide that this was God's best use of His possessions?" The reply back was, "Yes, but not to sell." And again, I responded "But, it's now his, he can do as he sees fit, hopefully as the Holy Spirit directs him," and then turning to the board members, I said, "If he had gotten into a wreck in it and the car was totaled, would you be mad at him? Of course not, because it belongs to him now and is his responsibility to manage as God directs." That seemed to end the conversation, but not their hearts' anger. There was always a suspicion of that particular staff member's motives from that time forward.

What I saw was how God used this incident to reveal the heart of the board. They had hidden strings, hidden expectations on the "gift." It seems it was NOT freely given. As I have mentioned, we have a life to give generously in response to a generous God. Most people think of giving in terms of time, talent and treasure. But I think there are five components to how God wants us to freely and generously give.

Please see **Figure 4-1. The Three Areas of My Life** (next page), as we discuss its contents here.

Time:

Each of us has 24 hours per day, every day of the year, and a finite number of years to live on this earth. None of us knows how many of those years we have. So, we are instructed to be concerned with the day we have before us, today. This is because our life may be demanded of us tomorrow. This thought alone should be sobering to us. Time is the only thing we have to give that we are given in limited supply. The idea of limited time should make us prioritize it very carefully. (Matt 6:34)

Talent:

Our talents – those natural gifts and "spiritual gifts," (*i.e.*, the specific abilities to do certain things well) with which we are blessed, are also unique gifts of God. They are part of the way we are created and they benefit the work God calls us to do in both the world and in the church. They were created for and in us, before the time that we should use them. Their work products go beyond the works of our hands to the works of our mind – which, in today's vernacular, are referred to as our "intellectual property." While our natural gifts can fit into our career, vocation, or "calling" in the world, our spiritual gifts are given to be used within the Body of Christ only, recognizing that each of us has a role in His church in which to utilize those talents. (1 Pet 4:10, 1 Cor 12)

Treasure:

Money and possessions are deceiving elements in the life of a Christian. The world system often confuses us because we have used our talent, and then traded the works of our hands or our intellectual property to acquire all that we have. We worked hard for what we have and, because we earned it through our hard work, we think it's ours to enjoy. Somewhat ironically, even if we were given what we have from a family member or gotten it by "luck," like a lottery ticket, we apply the same deceived logic. We wrongly credit it to the hard work of our

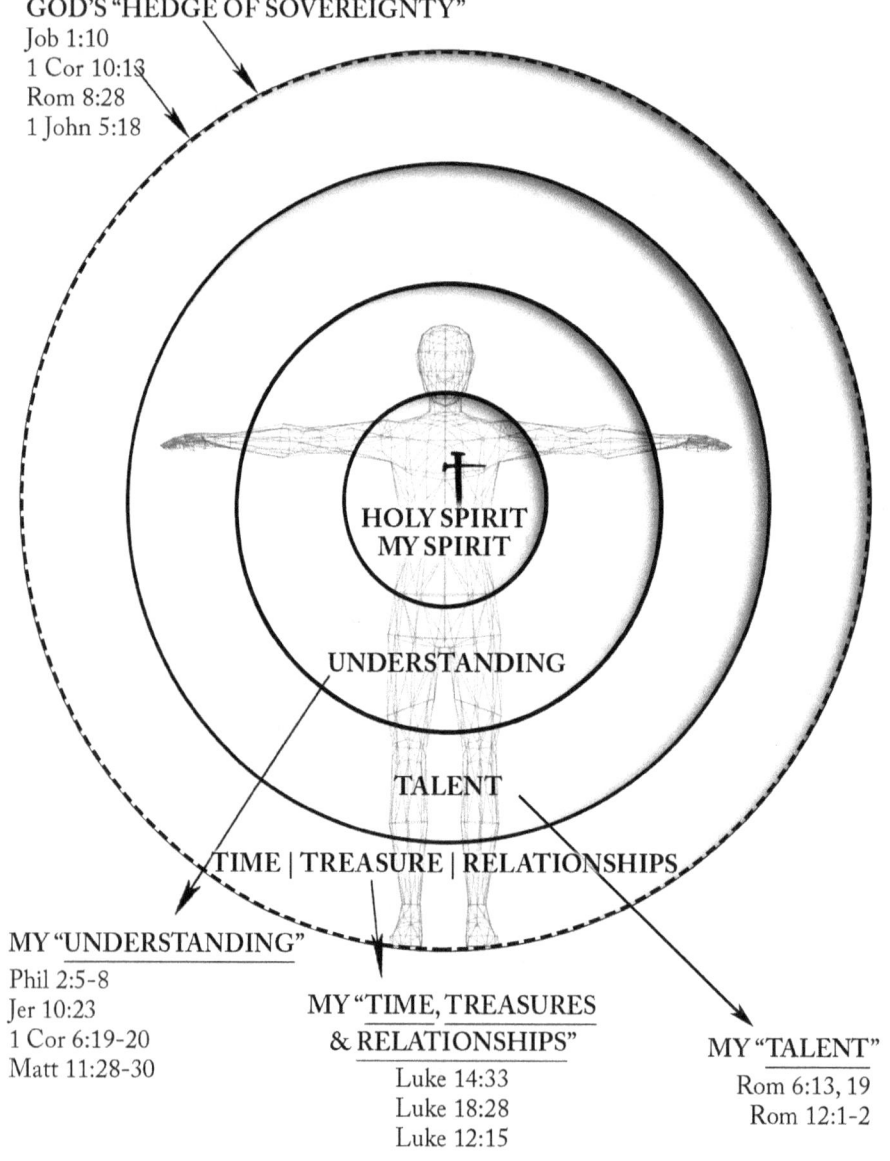

Figure 4-1

family, or our superior intellect in picking great lottery numbers, *etc.* We wrongly believe that we've earned what we have. The truth is, *all* we possess (past, present, future) is God's, for He has provided it for us to manage on His behalf. Our business, job, trust fund, or lottery winnings are just the venue through which He brought His possessions into our care. (2 Cor 8:7)

Understanding:

The revelation of God's will to us is also a gift to us from God. Biblical understanding revealed by the Holy Spirit is different from intellectual property that we produce on our own. It is what God has revealed to you about Himself. (1 Pet 1:1-9; 2 Pet 2:7) This understanding has been given to you to share with others, (Titus 2:11-15; Acts 11:23) – not to keep to yourself, or for your own edification, alone. (Heb 10:24-25) Instead, these jewels are to be given to those around you in order to bless and equip each other. (1 Thess 5:11-15) It's your stewardship responsibility – your *job* – to share your understanding generously and to grow in Christ with it. (1 Cor 9:6-10) And it's the Holy Spirit's job to give the understanding in the first place. (2 Cor 9:6-15; 1 Cor 3:5-9)

Relationships:

We have special gifts that at times are more valuable than all the others. Things such as love, empathy, forgiveness, compassion, sorrow, laughter, encouragement (Heb 10; 1 Thess 5:11-15) and many others that are the unique elements of relating, one-to-another, which are all gifts that God generously shares with us and that are to be just as generously shared by us with others. In the past, when people rallied around me in my greatest times of need, they didn't mention my gifts of money, time, or my leadership or teaching skills. They mentioned something more valuable to them – the times when they cried and I cried with them, when they grieved over a death and I held their hand quietly, or they poured it all out and I just listened. Emotional encouragement is what resonates in the heart and it seems to be what people need most. Ultimately, perhaps the only thing we do that builds the eternal, is building up the body of Christ.

Vertically, we have a relationship with God, through Jesus Christ. (Rev 7:15; Rev 14:5; Heb 4:14; Matt 26:3; Dan 5:7; Lev 13:3; Lev 13:36; Psa 24:7; Psa 24:9; Psa 24:10; 1 Pet 4:14; Col 3:3; Psa 42:11; Psa 43:5)

Horizontally, we have a relationship with His body – the people around us. (1 Cor 4:1-3, 21)

Stewardship

All that we have in our lives is given to us by God to steward. (Col 1:15-29) A steward is trusted to manage, invest, expend, and otherwise be accountable for the preservation, safety, disposition, or growth of an asset while under his care or until its return to its rightful owner.[1] It's a tremendous responsibility to be a steward of God's great and generous gifts and possessions. (Rom 9:21; Col 1:25; 1 Tim 5:17)

> "IT'S A TREMENDOUS RESPONSIBILITY TO BE A STEWARD OF GOD'S GREAT AND GENEROUS GIFTS AND POSSESSIONS."

This responsibility comes with great rewards. (Matt 5:12; Luke 6:23) Let's explore God's expectations of our stewardship.

To begin, get yourself out of the way by just accepting these truths:
- You don't own anything.
- Nothing that you have or can do comes to you apart from God's generosity to you. (Psa 95:3-7; Eph 2:8-10)
- All the components of generosity I just described were given to you by God to *manage* – not to *possess*. (Rom 14:7-12)
- You have been placed in charge over them to wisely and cautiously use them to expand their owner's (God's) kingdom. (Matt 20: 1-16)

Done?

Good. Now we can move on.

Understand that:
- You will be accountable for all with which you have been entrusted. (Rom 14:12) One day, you will stand before

---
1 https://www.biblestudytools.com/dictionary/steward/

God to explain why you invested His time, talents, treasure, understanding, and relationships the way you did. (2 Cor 5:10; Heb 9:27; Matt 25:14-30)
- Good stewards are trustworthy and endeavor to manage their Master's affairs in a manner pleasing to their Master, waiting with expectation for His imminent return. (2 Tim 4:8)
- No matter how long it takes, you are to be faithful – even unto death. (Rev 2:10-11)
- You are to remain hard at work and full of wisdom in the affairs of your Master, investing wisely for the best return for Him. (Titus 1:7; 1 Pet 4:10) You are not merely to save and conserve. (Eph 5:15-21; 2 Cor 9:6-8)

God has given us specific expectations on how to handle all we are in charge of. (2 Tim 3:16-17; Heb 4:11-13) We know we serve a generous God, and that His reward will also be generous. (Rev 2:7, 10, 17, 26-29; 3:5,6,10; Matt 5:12; Luke 6:23) Conversely, if we are unfaithful, we will experience **loss**. *I learned about such loss the hard way.*

THE HAITI PROJECT EXPERIENCE

In January 2010, there was a terrible earthquake in Haiti. Over a million people died or were left homeless, and it appeared it would take many years to bring relief to this island nation. Along with many other non-profits and Christian ministries, I was called upon to explore the possibility of providing permanent, yet affordable, housing in Haiti.

Over the subsequent months, we founded a non-profit organization and began exploring several options to produce a housing system that could be built either in the United States or in Haiti. We finally came up with a concept to assemble a network of volunteers from churches and businesses across America who would build houses in "kit form" to be transported and assembled in Haiti. The project would create villages with all of the social services and job opportunities needed to make each village viable for the long term.

I was appointed as this new non-profit's volunteer board chairman, and my wife and I contributed heavily. We ceded most of our office space, computers, phone system, and much of the hard costs of the startup. We spent our own time and gave of our relationships in order to share the vision throughout the Christian and corporate community. Eventually, we hired a CEO to run the operation, who was a "friend" experienced in building and developing communities. He brought his sister in to act as the business operations manager.

In preparation for assembling a community of these homes, our CEO had traveled to Haiti earlier in the year. While there, he explored the logistics of securing property in Haiti for construction, shipping the home kits, building on-site utilities, and basically everything we would need to put these villages where they would be needed to house the refugees made homeless by the earthquake. After several days in Haiti, our CEO returned with news that exceeded our greatest expectations. He had found a partner who had the land and virtually everything needed to develop enough property to place 5,000 homes. He returned with photos and topographical relief maps to demonstrate that it was all we had hoped for and beyond.

It was now time to take it on the road.

We held a series of community meetings throughout Nevada and Texas, which led to kick-off meetings where we demonstrated the house and presented our vision to the community leaders. Right away, several large churches signed up to have builds in their parking lots, and the project attracted the interest of large corporate sponsors and individual donors. Like a rocket lifting off the launch pad, this massive relief project began to rise.

Then came the explosion.

While in Las Vegas, I received a disconcerting email. It was from our Haitian partner. Its content led me to believe that the property in Haiti, upon which we relied, was not as secure as presented to us by our CEO. Prior to this email, I had witnessed some other disturbing behavior from our CEO. From the day he took the reins of leadership, he exhibited strife with the other team members, including bullying and a lack of follow-through. In addition, one of his subordinates accused him of lying, and other indications followed.

A Nevada philanthropist called and told me to never again send the CEO to her office. From her description, the CEO's behavior during his presentation was so bizarre that my philanthropist friend felt extremely uncomfortable. In Texas, the CEO failed to show up for an arranged meeting with the executive team of the largest church

Chapter 4: What is Generosity?

denomination in the state. He was also a "no-show" at the largest Christian radio station in Dallas, Texas, whose manager had requested an interview to find out more regarding the Haiti houses.

The Holy Spirit had shown me my poor stewardship, as revealed by all of these red flags, and many more warnings, and had given me opportunity after opportunity to correct it. But I ignored the warnings and rationalized them away.

> **"I IGNORED THE WARNINGS AND JUSTIFIED THEM AWAY."**

That is until an email arrived from our contractor in Haiti in regard to the property. If it was true that we actually didn't have the property secured in Haiti, then the project was in deep trouble. Our CEO and our staff, including me, had been traveling the country representing that we had already secured property in Haiti on which to build 5,000 homes.

Upon returning to the office, I began digging through the financial records. Shocked, I found falsified expense reports completed by the CEO's sister (our business manager) payable to the CEO. I also found the payroll taxes hadn't been paid. But most alarmingly, I discovered that the CEO, his sister, *and* the previous company that they had managed were currently under criminal investigation in Florida, where they lived prior to moving west. His sister alone had 50 felony warrants out for her arrest in Florida for financial maleficence.

It became clear that my worst nightmare was now a reality. There was no property. It all was a total fabrication and our CEO and his sister needed to be fired. The Board of Directors completely agreed, and I decided the task would need to be done upon my return from a business trip.

Another concern raised its head. Just before I left for California, I transferred monies from our general account to payroll. Yet within a few hours of that transfer, employees were simultaneously calling my cell and emailing me that our CEO refused to release payroll. His reason? There was no money. With that statement, he sent everyone home without being paid.

Then came the calls from sponsors, vendors, partners, and interested parties. The CEO had closed the project doors, contacted everyone he could and stated the project was "a bust," and claimed he had "discovered improprieties," even though he never stated specifically what those were. He took those actions completely without notice to, or consultation with, the Board.

Finally, after much avoidance, I was able to schedule a meeting with the CEO and his sister to terminate them both. They were both offered a severance package if they would agree to cease contact with all interested project parties. They refused, with the CEO saying, "God wants me to take you down!" Little did I know the lengths to which his pride and arrogance would take him to fulfill that threat.

We recruited a new CEO and began to pick up the pieces. Our first few builds were just weeks ahead.

In the meantime, the fired CEO had reached out to many local news outlets. Each had generally been reporting positively about our efforts to help the Haitians and refused to entertain his spin. Finally, the ex-CEO found one reporter willing to swallow his story. She began a narrative that was carefully crafted with no facts and a tremendous amount of innuendo. Just hours before she went to press, she contacted our office for comment. The new CEO responded to the reporter's request for comment, but the reporter wanted to speak directly to me, not the new CEO.

It turned out the article was not about our effort to help the Haitians but was a hit piece about me personally. The next day's front-page headline read:

FEDS WANT HAITI MONEY BACK

There it was in 18-point type, bold print: the lie that eventually ended the hopes for thousands of Haitians.

Eventually, the Haiti project was ruined by the erroneous media coverage. When it became apparent it could go no further, we closed it down without building one single house for the Haitians. The IRS thoroughly investigated that project as well, concluding there was no violation of the law and wrote a disinclination letter of prosecution to end the investigation. One man's arrogance and pride destroyed the hopes of some of the neediest people on planet earth.

THE HHS GRANT TRIAL

Buried within this irresponsible reporter's "FEDS WANT

HAITI MONEY BACK" headline and articles was an undifferentiated allusion to an ongoing legal dispute I had with the Department of Health and Human Services (HHS). This dispute was over a government grant that my *for-profit* business received in 2007, some three years before the Haiti earthquake! HHS wanted all the money returned, regardless of the fact we had conducted the activities of the grant in earnest. We appealed their decision, eventually winning the lawsuit against HHS, which embarrassed the local Department of Justice office. Having lost, they asked the IRS to investigate all of my business dealings, which they diligently scrutinized for the next several years. The IRS looked at every check, deposit, and financial transaction made in the prior ten years by *every* business I owned, into all of my personal affairs, and eventually, into the Haiti Project, as well (in which I was strictly, an unpaid volunteer).

All of the actual civil HHS lawsuit proceedings had happened long before the earthquake in Haiti, the formation of the non-profit Haiti Project, and the launch of its allied relief effort. Those facts made no difference to the reporter or the editor in all of their subsequent unfair and erroneous articles with which they continually hammered the Haitian Project.

The HHS-IRS investigative tsunami finally resulted in my indictment on criminal charges related to the HHS grant. Why? The prosecutor made it clear: he wanted me to drop the civil case against HHS so that the government wouldn't be required to pay potentially millions of dollars which we would be awarded when we won the HHS lawsuit.

In the months leading up to the criminal trial, the media relentlessly reported on every detail of the case's pre-trial development – some true, some made up, all curiously-sourced, and sometimes, even reporting on the Court's decisions before my attorneys were advised.

I was made out to be a charity fraudster, con artist, and a shyster over the Haiti project. In the midst of the firestorm, I lost much of my other business, most of my 'friends,' my reputation was destroyed, and I had a heart attack. None of "the conversation" was even related to the subject matter of the criminal investigation that led to the trial! The trial was actually about my alleged theft of government money (the grant) and tax evasion related to the HHS contract, which had concluded three years earlier!

All along the path leading to the trial, the federal government offered me one deal after another. But, the first condition of every deal offered was that I had to drop the civil suit against HHS. And each time these conditioned deals were offered, I refused this condition and the deal-offer because I would have to admit to doing something I didn't do. At one point I weakened, agreeing to plead "no contest," which would not require me to admit to committing a crime. Then the federal prosecutor refused. So, we went forward with the trial. My legal team requested a change in venue, asking the judge to hold the trial away from the intense, local media coverage in this small town. The Federal Court refused.

The trial began the next Monday, and the legal contest unfolded over the next five days. Eventually, both sides rested late Friday evening and the jury returned the following Monday for their deliberations. All week, my trial was in the headlines and none of the coverage was positive. The same reporter continued to paint me as being a danger to the public. The reporting continued through the weekend, with a Sunday Edition special feature. Even though none of the charges were public and no individual citizens were victims, I was, nevertheless, accused in the newspaper of being the worst of the worst, *stealing money* from *families* for *my own gain*.

Monday morning, after instructions from the Judge, the jury was released to deliberate. While they had nearly 40,000 documents to review, there was not one check, tax return, money transfer, or even a single deposit either signed or authorized by me that was in question. In other words, there was no evidence of wrongdoing or intent of wrongdoing. Yet, after a brief, 40-minute deliberation, the jury found me guilty.

As we moved into the penalty phase of the trial, God's hand moved mightily. The prosecution demanded a sentence of 7 to 10 years of prison time. At that daunting prospect, my wife and I decided we needed another attorney, someone who specialized in this area of penalty and appeal. My new attorney took the next year to very brilliantly negotiate with the prosecution over the "enhancements" that the prosecutors had asserted to support their demand for my sentencing. Eventually, he worked out something I had never heard of, a post-conviction agreement, in which, if I dismissed the civil lawsuit against HHS and agreed to never appeal my case, the prosecution would agree that I should only get 30 months in a federal prison camp. I signed the agreement and realized for the first time in all of the years of fighting my cases that – despite the tough circumstances at hand – I was now free to live and move on.

THE RESULTS

As I have shared my story over the years, I have heard many comments.

Some say, "Mike, you must have done something wrong, God doesn't let innocent people go to jail." Well, may I suggest you reread your Bible? It's chock-full of people who were unjustly imprisoned, their lives destroyed, and many even put to death after being falsely accused.

Putting that aside, I think the more important question is: "What did God display through this experience?" Frankly, He showed me grace in huge measure – much more than I could have imagined. Here I was, given an undistracted two and a half years to pray, think, and receive revelation about His purpose for my life having been turned upside down as it was … and it all boils down to stewardship.

> **"HE SHOWED ME GRACE IN HUGE MEASURE …"**

"Stewardship?" I will show you what I mean. Take a look at the stewardship parables of Jesus.

Let's begin with the parable of the shrewd manager in Luke 16:1-13. This parable is often called the "parable of the unrighteous steward," and it concerns an owner firing his business manager for wasting his assets. But, just before this steward's termination takes effect, he seems to trade favors with his master's debtors for a reduction in their debt. This parable is a hard one to understand. Many commentaries offer different explanations, but here is how it was applied in my life.

I was seeking the favor of those around me because I failed to heed the clear warning signs that this CEO was "integrity challenged." I reasoned the warnings away, even spiritualizing them as an act of love by ignoring what the Holy Spirit was showing me. I didn't want to stop the Haiti project's progress, which would have certainly happened if I had acted immediately. I mismanaged the relationships around me by not taking action. By my decision to NOT take any action, I ultimately hurt many, including hundreds of supporters, my family, my reputation, thousands of homeless Haitians, and the name of the Lord. As a result, my Master terminated me from my position as steward over His relationships in that project.

Now let's look at the parable of the talents in Matthew 25:14-30 and consider that I was entrusted with many different financial assets, relationships and understandings – all talents for which I was held accountable to my Master, the owner of those items. I wasn't preparing for the imminent return of my Master. Instead, I had an "it'll all work out" attitude. I didn't, and it didn't. I paid a big price for my poor stewardship.

Finally, the parable of the Ten Minas in Luke 19:11-27 shows that *many* people have comparable gifts. I actually believed that God somehow needed *me* to see this project through. (I am embarrassed to write these words now.) As a steward of my Master's property, I had a responsibility to faithfully invest His gifts in His Kingdom. By every account, I didn't. I let my Master down, and my misdirected stewardship will impact my position and reward in Heaven. (More on this concept later.)

I must admit it's hard to convey this story. In no way am I proud of my poor stewardship of the assets/gifts my Master entrusted to me, but I am thankful for His mercy and for what God did with and for me in the situation:

- Through the time I spent serving my negotiated sentence, I came closer to the Lord than I ever had been. I discovered a fresher intimacy with Him, and even had the opportunity to see and participate in real, spiritual revival in the institution where I served my prison time. God used me to write much of this book, which I pray He will use to bless others as greatly as He blessed me.
- I also learned to be a better steward of my body. After suffering my heart attack, my cardiologist said I would be disabled the rest of my life. My heart was severely damaged, and that damage could never be medically

reversed. While in federal prison, I learned to eat properly and began to exercise seriously. As a result, my head cleared. I was able to gain a much higher fitness level, one that I had not had since my thirties. The miraculous happened as God, "the Healer," (Isa 55:5-6; Psa 103:2-5) stepped in and, little-by-little, He reversed my heart's damage.

- God used me to disciple and train a great group of inmate-leaders who remain behind, still to serve Him as their sentences continue, as God has appointed.
- Today, there is little if any heart damage at all, and the lost years that were taken from me were "restored" seven-fold. (Joel 2:25-32; 1 Pet 5:10)

Both God and the devil wanted me to die; (John 3: 3-6; 1 Pet 5:8) but, for different reasons – and in different ways. Satan used slander, lies, and false accusations, in his attempt to destroy me. The Holy Spirit used those same lies to put my flesh and its vulnerability to the control of others in my life to death. The Lord used this season in my life to kill my desire for the praise of man. (1 Thess 2:4-6) Those criticisms by men worked God's will in my life to die – once and for all – to man's opinions. (Col 3:23-24) I now live solely for God. Sure, I'm accountable to a few close leaders, (Heb 13:17) – all of whom are Godly men – but I only seek to diligently please God – not man. (Col 3:23-24) It should, therefore, make no difference whether I offend man or please them because that is the Lord's business, not mine. I now choose to hide in the cleft of the Rock and allow Him to be my defense. (Ex 33:22) I now seek to rest in Jesus, and to live a life without reservation, generously, realizing I'm a work in progress and that – thankfully – God isn't finished with me yet. (Col 3:3)

> **"I GOT IN THE WHEELBARROW AND THE RIDE WAS AMAZING!"**

Honestly, though I wouldn't want to go through this again, I also wouldn't want to change one moment of those years. We serve a wonderful Master! I got in the wheelbarrow, and the ride was amazing! My hope is that my story of a particularly difficult season in my life will help you reflect on your own stewardship and your own life.

How are *you* doing? Do you treat everything in your life as if it belongs to your Master – its true Owner?

The Bible says,
- He owns the heavens and all the earth. (Deut 10:14; Lev 25:23)
- He is the ruler of all things. (1 Chr 29:11-12)
- Everything under heaven is His. (Job 41:11; Psa 24:1-2)
- All that is in the world is His. (Psa 50:10-12)
- All the gold and silver in the world is His. (Hag 2:8)

You will not find a single verse in scripture that allows you to claim any part of creation – including yourself – as belonging to you. First Corinthians 6:19-20 says you are not your own but were bought at a price. Not only does God own everything, He decides how much He will allow you to steward:
- He gives you the ability to produce wealth. (Deut 8:18)
- He decides who He makes poor or rich – don't just think money here. (1 Sam 2:7)
- Wealth and honor come from God. (1 Chr 29:12)

THE BOTTOM LINE:

If we really believe, I mean *wheel-barrow* believe, that all of the gifts He gives us: talents, money, possessions, relationships, understanding and time belong to God, shouldn't we be asking Him what *He* wants us to do with them? Shouldn't we ask often? Shouldn't we fearfully and faithfully be open to sharing any and all of those gifts as He directs? (1 Sam 13:13; Prov 3:5-6) Shouldn't we especially be asking to be directed to those who are in need of these gifts' use for their temporal (Matt 25:37-40) or eternal benefit (Matt 25:19-20)?

Still having trouble with the implications of being a steward? Is there something that comes to your mind for which it seems impossible to let go?

Pray this prayer aloud with me:

> *God, my Father, help me acknowledge that everything belongs to You.*
>
> *I confess that often I have imagined that You have given Your gifts to me as my own, to enjoy as I would, as though I am their ultimate recipient. Please forgive me and help me with the difficult areas of unbelief from this point forward.*
>
> *By faith, help me understand Your gifts as Your honored steward. By faith, help me do all that I can to: use them as You wish, distribute them as You direct, invest them as You desire, and keep and use only what You provide for me – ever-acting prayerfully and faithfully in Your name and employing Your gifts in Your love, for Your Kingdom, and to Your glory – and that I may enjoy You forever.*
>
> *Thank You, Lord, for another chance to serve You.*
>
> *In Jesus Name, Amen*

REPEAT AS NECESSARY

Chapter 5
THE IDOLATRY OF THIS AGE

There is an earthly gift that keeps on giving and keeps on giving you TROUBLE – it is called ***MATERIALISM***. Like so many earthly gifts that come our way, it is not given freely. Instead, it comes (as these all do) with strings attached and a price tag. Materialism is wrapped up with a pretty bow that says, "Open this and you will be satisfied in life!" It comes with a promise that this pretty gift will continue to give you the satisfaction, acceptance, significance, and security you need. Think about it. Every commercial you see on TV, the ad you read in a magazine, or see on the Internet basically says, "Buy this product and your life will be more satisfying!"

The beer commercial's blatant message says: Our product makes you more pleasing to pretty girls, if you drink a lot of it, you'll attract many pretty girls and be cool.

Playing to your need for acceptance and significance, the beer commercial is lying to you. A lot of beer makes you drunk, silly, and fat – none of which attracts pretty girls (well, not the kind you would want). But, as well-crafted advertising does, there is a secondary message. Girls, if you find a drunk, silly, fat guy, he'll find you pretty – playing to *your* need for security.

Referencing action figure dolls reminiscent of Mattel's G.I. Joe, Barbie, and Ken, the 1996 Nissan 300ZX commercial (another personal favorite, which you may remember) shows "G.I. Joe" driving up to the dollhouse in Nissan's shiny new convertible sports car. He honks, nods toward the car, and winks to "Barbie" who is out on the balcony, In the next scene, "Barbie" is in the passenger seat of the convertible driving off with "G.I. Joe," with the wind in her hair. "Ken" is now out on the balcony, with a tear in his eye.[1]

This message? Our car will get you the impossible dream, tearing the perfect girl away from the perfect boy in the perfect house – so *you* can be the perfect couple – in the perfect car (of course).

This commercial plays to our need for acceptance and security.

---
1 https://www.youtube.com/watch?v=9MlLlY28Kso and http://lab.tier10.com/2012/11/29/throwback-thursday-nissan-1996-200-million-ad-campaign/)

The Secondary Message? You are just like GI Joe – macho, attractive, and obviously smart – if you buy the right car. You are significant!

This, basically, is the hidden theme of the materialism message:

"MATERIALISM IS INVASIVE!"

It's invasive in the world, invasive in the church, in our families, and in our minds. Materialism has infected our entire existence and not just in the western culture. The materialism message is played via advertising worldwide through satellite TV, radio, movies, and merchandising. If you don't think so, then the next time you see a news report about a tragedy in the developing world, take notice of the desperately poor children wearing a hat or T-shirt embossed with a designer logo.

Some would say, "Mike that's a fake or bootlegged T-shirt." You have missed the point. These kids wear such T-shirts as their prized possession and for the hope provided by its message. They want to be rich, like the people they see in those commercials on TV, in the movies, or on the print ads and posters for those movies!

The idolatry of materialism has nothing to do with what you possess. It has everything to do with what you *want* and what you hope will fulfill your need for acceptance, significance, and security. This need, though, is something only GOD can fulfill through His Son, Jesus Christ. Materialism is the idolatry of this age. It is what the world bows down to and worships. We are so enamored with the pursuit of money and things. Even the church often leaves the Living God on the side of the road as it chases the latest 'shiny object' that would bring in new congregants.

A.W. Tozer puts it like this:
> *We in the churches seem unable to rise above the fiscal philosophy that rules the business world. So, we introduce into our church finances, the psychology of the great secular institutions so familiar to us all and judge a church by its financial support, much as we judge a bank or department store.*
>
> *A look into history will quickly convince any*

interested person that the true church has almost always suffered more from prosperity than from poverty.

The history of churches and denominations follow pretty closely a rather uniform pattern: It is to begin in poverty and power; get established to a degree that removes all hazard and give financial security; becoming accepted by society; outgrow the need for divine intervention; keep Christ as a figurehead, ignore His Lordship and carry on after the traditions of the elders; offer the clergy a reward for staying in line in the form of an old age pension; put enough persons in places of power who profit financially by prosperity of the group. After that it's REQUIESCAT IN PACE (a prayer for a peaceful repose of a dead person) and the tragic thing about it all is that no one knows he is dead.[2]

My friend, I have seen Tozer's sad description of this descent into idolatry first hand. It infects the church everywhere. In the years before I began writing, I served as a consultant to some of the most admired Christian ministries and churches in the world, as well as many hundreds of small ones. What I observed was neither confined to nor aligned with just one Christian philosophy or denomination or even country or geographic region. In my travels, its trappings and practice appeared across the board in the church, from Pentecostal to Baptist, suburban to urban inter-city, white, black, or Hispanic, the same thinking prevails.

More than once, I've dined with pastors in their private dining rooms, adjacent to their private offices, attended to by their private chef, waiter, or staff. I've sat with them in their town car motorcades – accompanied by their security and staff entourages who attend to the ministry leader's every need. One

> **"MORE THAN ONCE, I'VE DINED WITH PASTORS IN THEIR PRIVATE DINING ROOMS, ADJACENT TO THEIR PRIVATE OFFICES, ATTENDED TO BY THEIR PRIVATE CHEF, WAITER, OR STAFF."**

---

[2] The Warfare of the Spirit: Religious Ritual Versus the Presence of the Indwelling Christ, by A. W. Tozer, Harry Verploegh (Compiler), Moody Publishers, Chicago, June 2006.

such leader had matching black Cadillac Escalades with shiny rims and blacked-out windows. You would have thought a world leader or the latest Rap music star (or, perhaps, some underworld high-ender!) was arriving with such caravan transport and private security! And yes, add the private jet for world travel, and the five-star luxury hotel suites.

I have seen ministry leaders play with the offering numbers, evangelism numbers, and attendance numbers – always and invariably to demonstrate their "ministry success" while not even measuring what might be important to God's.

Privately, I have asked these leaders why they have chosen to conduct themselves this way. Their answer is always the same. "My people want to belong to a demonstrably successful ministry, and besides, If I don't keep and protect my image, I could lose everything."

What image? They are no more than just a man who, at times, is used by God. And, what are they going to lose? Money? Power? Prestige? None of those things belong to them, anyway.

Are we going to bow down to the living God and trust Him with our entire ministry?

Or instead, lean on Materialism, the Idolatry of this age?

Well, let's talk about how Materialism brings ruin to our lives and the ministries we serve.

Materialism destroys spiritual life

Being materialistic causes you to ignore God's intended uses for the five components He gives us to steward for His purposes and glory that we previously addressed. Instead of honoring God's intent, we choose position, possessions, feel-good relationships, and convenient understandings – and we choose to spend time, talent, and treasure pursuing those material things over the intimacy with God as our soul desires. It's a fruitless attempt to find acceptance, security, and significance apart from God. We become idolaters, like those in the Laodicean church rebuked by Jesus in Revelation 3:17-18 because they had earthly things, but were poor in the things of God. Just like the Laodiceans, it seems that materialism blinds us to our own spiritual poverty and the actual state of our spiritual maturity and health.

Jesus suggests that riches can be a spiritual liability. In the parable of the Rich Young Ruler, recorded in Mark 10:23-25, He tells about the difficulty the rich man has entering God's Kingdom. It's imperative to realize the cultural context of this parable. At the time, Godliness was equated to wealth as the outwardly observable trappings of blessing. It was thought that if you're wealthy, then you must have God's favor. This is still true today, as I found in my work with pastors. It is pervasive in our churches – far and wide.

> **"IT WAS THOUGHT THAT IF YOU'RE WEALTHY, THEN YOU MUST HAVE GOD'S FAVOR."**

The beggar, Lazarus, clearly received the blessing of God over the rich man who had lived in the lap of luxury all his life. In this passage, the phrase "poor man" actually means totally helpless. Lazarus was totally helpless before God, while the rich man wasn't so much. (Luke 16:19-31) This is not to say that God doesn't, can't, or won't love the rich, wealthy, popular, famous, or celebrated because He certainly does, can, and will. Nor that the rich, wealthy, popular, famous, or celebrated don't, can't, or won't love God. Many do. The problem is that the rich, wealthy, popular, famous, or celebrated have so many other things to love in addition to God or, more likely, *instead* of Him. This is why Jesus said you cannot serve God and money, or you'll end up loving your earthly things more than God, and you won't be able to even see it. (Matt 6:24)

Materialism leaves you in a state of fear and anxiety

The dread of living in uncertain and insecure circumstances – and the fear of those circumstances *changing* – produces anxiety. The more you have of anything such as money, possessions, relationships, understanding, or talents, the more you attempt to control and preserve them. However, there is never enough time to do this, nor can we provide enough protection to assure their preservation. We become uncertain, insecure, and anxious about our hold on them. When that insecurity becomes fully mature, and when the things we cannot control inevitably begin to slip away, we become fearful.

It is no wonder that in Matthew 6:19-34, Jesus' discourse on earthly and heavenly treasures, "Lay not up for yourselves treasures upon earth …" ends with His sharp, concluding distinction, drawn in verse 24 "…Ye cannot serve both God and mammon." But this is immediately followed by an admonition that speaks directly to this control issue. In Matthew's next nine verses, we are told to *NOT* worry about anything – especially about tomorrow – rather, we are told to set our hearts on things above, because to set your heart on materialism is to glorify yourself and not God. By so doing – even though saved – we are destined to perpetual insecurity, uncertainty, and anxiousness here on earth *and* to a dearth of reward in heaven. Closing his first letter to Timothy, the Apostle Paul instructs his disciple to command those who are rich in "this present world" not to put their hope in their wealth, but instead to put their hope in God who richly provides. (1 Tim 6:11-21, specifically, verse 17 and amplified in verses 18-19)

Materialism fails to satisfy

Materialism gives us a false "full" feeling. Like snacking on potato chips and soda, so materialism keeps us spiritually full but not spiritually satisfied. Buying things, wasting time, one-sided-relationships, using talents for earthly pursuits, and the like, keeps our lives hurried and distracted. These never fully satisfy becoming instead, a demanding treadmill of diminishing returns. The satisfaction of buying the new car lasts only as long as its new-car smell – seldom more than a few weeks after purchase. The new couple you wanted to have over for dinner disappoints you. After having spent hours of personal time preparing for that work-related presentation for your boss, it is discarded or ignored. But our response is often to do even more of the same: buy even more new stuff, meet even more new people, or work even harder. With each renewed effort, even temporary satisfaction becomes more elusive. Let me illustrate:

There was a young man with whom I used to spend time. Attending college, he spent much of his time studying and attending class. Each semester he would get a check for school expenses. It was a little more than he needed, but not so much that he could live beyond his very tight college budget. Each semester, when he got his check, he would go shopping – but always for stuff he *wanted*, not for things he actually *needed*. He justified this by reassuring himself "he deserved it" because he "could go months at a time without even the basics."

I remember one time when he spent weeks researching flat screen televisions, finally deciding on one at Costco. He even talked the store manager into a discount. He took it home and spent hours installing it – hiding all the wires in the walls, adjusting the surround sound speakers, and so-forth. Then, after just a few short days, he returned it all to the store. "Why?" I asked. He said that he had watched it a few days and it worked perfectly. The images on the screen were fantastic, and the sound was just like being there. "So, what's the problem?" I asked. He replied, "Honestly, after a couple of days, it just lost its newness, it wasn't cool anymore, so I'm going to buy a new cell phone or iPad." Which he did. Then, after having that item for a short time, he sold it for about a 50% loss. Why? Because it, too, had lost its "coolness."

Over the years, I watched him do the same kind of thing with cars, classes, animals, roommates, friends, girlfriends, and so on. Eventually, nothing satisfied the deeper need he had. With each attempt, it was harder to find the false fulfillment he would get for a few days. Everything lost its "coolness."

I find it interesting that in the final chapter in the Bible, Jesus says:

> Whoever is thirsty, let him come; and
> Whoever wishes, let him take the free
> gift of the water of life.
> – Revelation 22:17

Whatever it is that you may be seeking ... satisfaction for your soul will only be found in Christ.

All else leaves you wanting.

Materialism ignites the self-sufficiency of the old human nature

When you have it "all," and can see no more stuff to need, you begin to feel you've arrived, because, just about every earthly thing you want you can get, and so, where – or for what – do you need God?

Remember, faith requires perceived risk. If you have put your faith in yourself, your treasures, your relationships, your talents, your understanding, then where is your risk? Why do you need to pray if you have it all under control? Do you resort to prayer only in a last-ditch effort – when all the other resources you've tried have failed?

> **"REMEMBER, FAITH REQUIRES PERCEIVED RISK."**

Self-sufficiency will bring a slow death to your spiritual life and maturity as a Christian believer. It inhibits your generosity. You would think great wealth and prosperity would naturally bring great generosity. But what it truly does is insulate us from needs—our needs and the needs of others, which causes us to miss what God is doing around us, in us, and what He generously wants to do through us.

This self-sufficiency can lead to pride, (Prov 16:18) a pride that "I have achieved what I have achieved; because of my brilliant … (effort, talent, relationship, understanding – pick one)." We have a tendency to take the credit, be thankless, and remain full of ourselves. With pride resting in our hearts, we become judgmental toward those who have less than we do. We make statements like, "I am smarter, wealthier, more gifted, and more knowledgeable than that person or those types of people." It's what drives racism, sexism, and, yes, denominationalism. Self-sufficient pride wears like an old, worn-out, oversized, suit coat and we convince ourselves we look good in it, because, if we're honest, we'll need to be open and vulnerable with God and those around us. We would be revealing we are just not all we're cracked up to be – something everyone *else knows* (especially God), but apparently, *we don't*. (Prov 16:18-19)

> The Apostle Paul asked the church in Corinth:
> For who makes you different from anyone else? What do you have that you did not receive? And if you did receive it, why do you boast as though you did not?
> – 1 Corinthians 4:7

This self-sufficient pride will cause us to judge others unjustly. History is full of unjust governmental rulers, cult leaders, church leaders, and business leaders all of whom have made careers of putting down their followers and the general populace in order to lift themselves up. James warns the prideful that anyone who practices injustice to the poor will come under God's judgment, as he wrote in his letter!

> Now listen, you rich people, weep and wail because of the misery that is coming on you. Your wealth has rotted, and moths have eaten your clothes.

> Your gold and silver are corroded. Their corrosion will testify against you and eat your flesh like fire. You have hoarded wealth in the last days. Look! The wages you failed to pay the workers who mowed your fields are crying out against you. The cries of the harvesters have reached the ears of the Lord Almighty. You have lived on earth in luxury and self-indulgence. You have fattened yourselves in the day of slaughter. You have condemned and murdered the innocent one, who was not opposing you.
> – James 5:1-6 (NIV)

Today, we still contend with slavery, drug trafficking, addictions, sex trafficking, open prostitution, abortions, homosexuality, and many other shameful issues. They are all sinful or abominable before God. Some are contrary to civil order within society as God prescribed, while others are even contrary to mankind's survival. However, they are all now marching slowly forward toward civil and social acceptance, legality, and even to religious toleration and inclusion into full belief and practice. This is syncretism to the extreme!

Although never admitted as such, the reasons for their acceptance are accordingly justified for the financial gain or self-justification of those that promote them, and through the public acceptance of those who are consumers of or participants in such degrading products, services and practices.

We Christians are included, as we have turned a blind eye toward the materialism that drives such victimizing behavior. Instead of a deafening outcry against injustice and immorality by marching in the streets to end the slavery, the murder of innocent unborn babies, the exploitation of women and children, abominable sexual practices and their legitimization in "civil unions," we tacitly agree that the church should stay out of public discourse on these social issues. We tone down that "sin-talk stuff" and remain behind the closed doors of the church building – even as forceful, authoritative, Biblical preaching against such sin is increasingly characterized as "hate speech."

The church of Philippi had a similar problem.

The Apostle Paul and his companion, Silas went about freely

preaching the gospel until they met with a slave girl who earned a great deal of money for her owners. The problem was, she was also demon-possessed, and she followed and harangued Paul for his preaching. Annoyed, he cast the demon out of her, freeing her from this terrible curse. Her owners, however, rather than being relieved that their slave girl was healed, were furious that they had lost their meal ticket. As the Book of Acts reveals, it was the demon that had the supernatural fortune-telling abilities that this young slave girl demonstrated. Without its abilities to see the future, her customers left, and her owners stopped making money. (Acts 16:16-18)

> Paul's action did not turn out well.
> [When the owners of the slave girl] ... realized that their hope of making money was gone, they seized Paul and Silas and dragged them to the marketplace to face the authorities. They brought them before the magistrates and said, "These men are Jews, and are throwing our city into an uproar by advocating customs unlawful for us Romans to accept or practice."
> The crowd joined in the attack against Paul and Silas, and the magistrates ordered them to be stripped and beaten with rods. After they had been severely flogged, they were thrown into prison, and the jailer was commanded to guard them carefully. When he received these orders, he put them in the inner cell and fastened their feet in the stocks.
> – Acts 16:19-24 (NIV)

Materialism promotes immorality

My years in prison ministry taught me one thing: Almost everyone rightfully incarcerated there, is there because of materialism in some form or another. Drugs, sex trafficking, white-collar crime, and even violent crimes have a defining connection to a materialistic lifestyle that was, in the end, either being pursued or maintained through illegal means. In prison, it's common to hear stories about stacks of money, the finest cars and jewelry, sexual escapades, and mansions. I even listened to a man tell me about the private zoo he had where his main reason for committing one or more crimes was to buy another elephant. Why? So, he would have a pair of them!

What is sadder though, is that even after some of these men and women have been incarcerated for years and years, they incessantly carry on with grandiose stories about the life they once lived. They do so even after having lost everything because the government seized their possessions for restitution and now, they have barely enough money to buy toothpaste and shaving cream. It is complete self-delusion, living a life that is long gone. Some even keep pictures and news articles in a homemade scrapbook to "prove" they really are this person they say they are. All the while, they wear drab prison clothing and even have to wait for someone in charge to decide when they can use the restroom. Sound extreme? If you think materialism has not infiltrated your house, your church, your office, think again. It has infected us all. Even within my own company.

A few years ago, we held a ministry leadership workshop in the Midwest. Picture this: a room full of pastors, business leaders, and ministry supporters gathered together to learn how to help their organization be more generous. The first session of the day is about materialism, and part of the teaching hit pretty hard on materialism and manipulation. After that first session, our presenter offered the participants a chance to purchase some additional material for a low price, "only available while at the workshop."

Later that week I received a gracious, but very poignant, email about that pitch. In his rather ironic way, the sender pointed out the manipulation of our offer. Why, if the price was a good price, is it only available while at the workshop? Clearly it was a sales pitch, a ploy, to push attendees to buy books!

He was right. That is exactly what it was – the marketers' old favorite: the "scarcity" sales pitch!

I would have liked to blame the presenter and his oversight or pretended I didn't receive the email, but I did receive it, and I had personally trained the presenter. Materialism had not only infected my company, but it had infected me, as well. All I could do was agree with the sender, apologize, and have all of our training materials reprinted without the "offer." I was embarrassed.

It was a valuable lesson to learn. I believe we all need to seriously realize that materialism, the idol of this generation, works hard to infiltrate our lives, churches, businesses, and relationships.

> **"MATERIALISM IS THE IDOL OF THIS GENERATION."**

We are saturated with its message that worldly happiness comes from being surrounded with cool stuff, fabulous people, superior positions and their titles, and the power of celebrity that makes people serve our desires. It is a demanding, never-ending, treadmill of acquire-and-discard that results in a lack of fulfillment, acceptance, significance, and security. It always leaves us hollow inside.

Recently, I saw a reference to an automaker's advertisement that read,

> **"You can't buy happiness**, but now you can *lease* it!"

Let me ask you, is this what your life has been reduced to?

Or, can you live a life of joy and contentment (1 Tim 6:6-12) knowing you are a child of God. (Luke 6:35; Rom 8:16-17)

The Apostle Paul wrote to the church at Philippi that he learned how to be content in whatever circumstance he found himself. Whether in prosperity or by humble means, abundance or hunger, being filled or suffering; he could (and we can!) "do all things through Christ, who strengthens me!" (Phil 4:11-13) Paul would know. He had a life of abundance, education, and status. (Phil 3:4-6) He also had a life of hardship, suffering, and persecution. (2 Cor 11:23-33) Yet, he was content, knowing Who God is and Whose he was. This *knowing* – this revelation – brings joy, not happiness, into our lives.

Happiness vs. Joy

I have noticed a growing trend in the confusion between happiness and joy and how it has crept into our lives. I had a couple of long-time pastor-friends who had committed their lives to the service of God's people. Each was married for over ten years and free from disqualifying sin in their lives that would take them away from full-time ministry. However, both families came apart: husbands losing wives and blaming themselves for it, children losing mothers and blaming themselves for it, and wives choosing to leave and losing their families, their children, and their husbands, all for the sake of – "happiness."

The first of these pastor-friends had a beautiful family with all the ensuing fun of vibrant boys. They lived and served in an awesome rural community. They had a nice family home on a few acres where they could have some animals, a pleasing and fruitful garden, and a peaceful, idyllic life.

The wife was very lovely, tall, and healthy and was a great mother to the boys. But life started to unravel for her. She became discontent with all she had been blessed with. She began to feel like she was missing out, though on what, she wasn't so certain. She decided to take up a hobby – scuba diving, of all things, considering she lived more than a six-hour drive from the ocean. Eventually, she began to take trips to Hawaii to complete her dive training. Then she would continue her personal goal by traveling alone to "acquire more dive time."

You might be asking, "Did she meet someone else?"

Yes, she did, but it wasn't another man.

It was, in her words, "happiness."

Throughout this period, she would have long phone conversations with her mother, who had been married several times herself. Her mom seemed to have one message for her daughter, "You deserve to be happy." Her mom encouraged her to pursue whatever would make her happy, whatever it took. While it is unclear whether her daughter expressed unhappiness in life first, or her mother introduced the idea that the daughter appeared "unhappy," regardless, this confusion entered the daughter's thinking.

One day, she returned from a diving trip and informed her husband she was moving out. Did she move to Hawaii? Did she move in with a new boyfriend? No. Instead, she rented an apartment a few miles away so the kids could come visit. A few months passed, and she was still not happy. Too many things in her hometown reminded her of her unhappiness. With this final revelation, she moved to California to live near the beach, effectively abandoning her family. The result of this abandonment was severe on her family. The confusion, hurt, and betrayal her husband and boys experienced was immeasurably devastating. Her boys felt responsible for their mother's abandonment. The sense of loss scarred them for life. Her husband lost his job at the church and eventually the family dream home he'd built. It was all too much to hold together.

Did she ever find happiness? I doubt it. Last I heard, she had given up diving and found another man living in a rural area. This time, there was no commitment and, consequently, no marriage. They decided just to live together to see if it might work. Happiness ... still eluding her.

My other pastor-friend was married for over two decades. All the while, his wife was active in the church, active with the youth, and active with other women in the church. She was always smiling, laughing, and engaged, casting the illusion she was content. On the outside, her life had an appearance of "normal." On the inside, there was a growing discontentment.

As their children reached adulthood, they began to live their own lives. She tried finding happiness with foster children. And when that didn't work, she slowly began living a separate life, dropping out of all her usual activities. Her new life began to look more like a college kid's lifestyle, one who just moved out of their parents' house for the first time.

She began frequenting bars and concerts, even taking vacations, all without her husband. Not unexpectedly, she became depressed,

> **"SHE BEGAN FREQUENTING BARS AND CONCERTS, EVEN TAKING VACATIONS, ALL WITHOUT HER HUSBAND."**

as none of these activities made her happy. Finally, the crushing realization came. She was an unhappy middle-aged woman, and the revelation was too much for her. She moved out of her home, abandoning her husband and family, leaving behind the facade of the counterfeit "good life" she had been living. The last I heard of her, she was living on the streets ... homeless. "Happiness" – having deserted her completely.

As you can imagine, her endless pursuit of 'happiness' never paid off. As with the first wife's story, moving away from her problems as her solution—was, maybe, no solution after all.

What do these two lives, these two stories, have in common? On the outside, everything seemed perfect, but inside these two women had a raging conflict. They had everything that should have made them happy, including loving husbands, wonderful families, stability, financial freedom, and plenty of free time to pursue their interests.

Some would say the husbands didn't attend to their wives as they should have. Perhaps. Yet I personally know both of these families. The husbands did everything they could think to do toward saving their dying relationships. But, from my observation, I compare what they went through to a spouse watching helplessly as their partner succumbed to Alzheimer's. In these cases, they were watching a different disease – their wives' ever accelerating pursuit of the diminishing returns of "happiness." With it came a slow, but steady, degradation of their relationship from what they had once enjoyed.

> **"DAILY, MORE PAIN WAS THRUST UPON EACH HUSBAND AS THE BRIDE OF HIS YOUTH SLIPPED AWAY BEFORE HIS VERY EYES."**

Daily, more pain was thrust upon each husband as the bride of his youth slipped away before his very eyes. Each wife chose to forget the life that had once excited them together, deciding, somehow, a better, happier life was just outside the front door of the home they had built with their spouse. Instead, only an ever-increasing numbness crept in to replace all they established and realized as a loving, Godly family.

Here's the problem: Our society, the world, the flesh, and the devil (1 John 2:16) are all selling a cheap imitation of the joy of Christ. (2 Tim 4:1-5; 1 Tim 6:3-4)

It's called "happiness!"

Happiness comes from the Latin root word [*felīcitās*]. It's also the root word for "happen," a word that is tied to circumstance – so, the *circumstance* in which we find ourselves, becomes the indicator, the provider, or even the creator, of our *happiness*.

I realized this on a day when I was in the middle of laughing and playing with my two young boys. We were having a water pistol fight in the house! And, we were having so much fun – even under the mildly disapproving, yet smiling, looks we got from my wife – which made it *all the more* fun! As I ran across our den, avoiding a particularly wet crossfire from my squealing boys, I caught my bare little toe on the wooden leg of the couch.

In a flash, I went from "fun and laughter" to "pain and anguish!"

My attitude, my mood, even my actions *all changed* – almost before I hit the floor – grasping my instantly-throbbing toe. In a slim tenth-of-a-second, I no longer cared about the fun I'd been having with my two boys, no longer cared how wet I was, who was winning, or what my wife was thinking. I was totally focused on just one thing: the throbbing in my toe.

The laughter stopped as everyone became concerned for me. Of course, the pain quickly subsided. What I noticed most, though, was that my joy quickly returned.

Despite the fact that I lost the toenail within a few days and I had to walk tenderly on that foot, that day is ingrained in my memory as one of the greatest days of my life. Even with the changing circumstances from fun to pain (which soon faded away), the contentment of being a father, and the byproduct of joy that it brings, is ever-present with me now.

Joy is much more than circumstantial. It lies deep in our hearts. (Rom 15:13) It's rooted in whom and Whose we are, knowing that in Christ alone, we have salvation and deliverance. (John 10:7-9; Act 4:11-12; 1 Pet 4:5) Truly, you can know His mercy and faithfulness to you, your family, and the world (Lam 3: 22, 23) – Christ is our victorious warrior (Zeph 3: 17), and in Him, we have the victory, (Zeph 3: 17) all the time, even among the toughest of battles. (1 John 5:4) He makes us complete, saves us from the penalty, pollution, power, and, ultimately, the presence of sin. (1 John 5:4)

> **"JOY IS MUCH MORE THAN CIRCUMSTANTIAL. IT LIES DEEP IN OUR HEARTS."**

That joy is seen by those around us, and goes out even to the ends of the earth, as God gets the glory. (Matt 5:14-16)

In THIS, we find contentment, (1 Tim 6:6-8) not in what we have done, or the circumstances we are in, and not in those circumstances we've made up to be happy, but solely because we are found in the life of Christ. (Col 3:1-4) And being in Christ brings overwhelming contentment (1 Tim 6:6-8) and the by-product of Godly contentment, (Phil 4: 10-13) which is joy. (Matt 14:25-31) Just knowing our lives are all His and that no matter what we have, where we are, what we are doing or going through, HE has our best interests at heart. (Matt 6:25-34) There is no greater joy! (3 John 1:4)

Happiness comes and goes with changing circumstances, but the joy of contentment found in Christ remains. (Phil 4: 11-13, I Tim 6: 6-12) It's this contentment and the resulting joy that delivers us from materialism. (1 John 2:16-17; 1 Pet 4:5) Knowing Whose we are, and who God is, is the only thing that gives us acceptance, significance, security and fulfills all we desire.

In his book, *The Pursuit of God*,[3] A.W. Tozer encourages us to pray:

> *Father, I want to know Thee, but my cowardly heart fears to give up its toys. I cannot part with them without inward bleeding, and I do not try to hide from Thee the terror of the parting. I come trembling, but I do come. Please root from my heart all those things which I have cherished so long and which have become a very part of my living self, so that Thou mayest enter and dwell there without rival. Then shall my heart have no need of sun to shine in it, for Thyself wilt be the light of it, and there shall be no night there.*
>
> *In Jesus' name. Amen.*

---

3 Pursuit of God, By: A.W. Tozer, Bethany House Publishers.

Chapter 6
INVESTING IN OUR ETERNITY

Have you ever watched the opening ceremonies of the Olympic games on television? I love the opening event because it gives me a real sense of the magnitude of the games along with the flavor of the hosting country. It begins with a procession of the athletes, each representing their own nation, proudly carrying their country's flag, laughing and taking selfies, capturing for themselves the most exciting moment of their lives. Think of the years of training, the competitions, the hard-won victories, and the painful losses each athlete experienced to get to this place in their lives. Imagine the incredible pride they have in their hearts. Even when they realize that they will most likely not be a medal contender, they are still proud just to just be in the games themselves and to be identified as an *Olympic Athlete*.

There is another group, one that is harder to see on television. It's the audience. You can see flashing cameras, all the way up to the last row, and hear the deafening roar of cheers and applause. I have been in large sports arenas where every seat is filled. It's a surreal experience. Picture yourself in the audience during the opening ceremonies. Imagine the effort you made to get there,

> **"YOU CAN SEE THE FLASHING CAMERAS, ALL THE WAY UP TO THE LAST ROW, AND HEAR THE DEAFENING ROAR OF CHEERS AND APPLAUSE."**

including the expense and sacrifice, even if you were in the "cheap seats" – you know, the last row behind a pole! You're so far from the actual procession that you can barely see it. Nevertheless, you are just as excited to be there. Maybe you're there for the love of the games, or to cheer on a friend, but now that you're there, you are thrilled. What's interesting to note is from the athletes' perspective, under the bright lights of the field, most of the audience is in the dark. They only know their presence by the cheering sounds and the flashing of cameras. But the audience can see every competitor's flag. The only item inhibiting the detail of their view is the distance from the field to their seats (and that darned pole).

And though they long to be closer, they are still glad to be right where they are.

What about the athletes who are there, but didn't make the Olympic team? I bet they wish they had trained a little harder, or run a few tenths of a second faster in order to be down on the field, instead of sitting in the seats with the audience. Yet they, too, are still glad to be there along with the workers and officials, entertainers and volunteers. Then, there are many who are outside the stadium, who can hear the cheers, see the lights radiate above the stadium, and who, though out there in the dark and wish they were inside, are glad to be where they are, too. It's too late for them now, and they've missed their opportunity to be inside to watch the games.

So why do I share this moment with you? I think that it illustrates what you and I, as Christians, look forward to when one day we stand before the Lord.

Our Final Examination

The Bible mentions two judgments that will happen after we die or if we are taken up in the rapture. (Rev 20:11-15, 2 Cor 5:10)

First, there is the Great White Throne Judgment. (Rev 20:11-15) This judgment is the one most of us have heard about, because of all those evangelists' sermons designed to encourage you out of your life of sin and propel you down the aisle in pursuit of your salvation at the altar call. We often think of the Great White Throne Judgment as the "heaven or hell thing" for us Christians, but it's really not that. It's a time of reckoning for those who are *not* found to be in Christ. (Rev 20:15)

You see, Christ paid the price of our sin for us. We are His, and He testifies to this and to the fact of our relationship with Him to the Judge on the Great White Throne (Himself). So, we Christians get skipped over on this one.

Those who do not get skipped over are the ones not found in Christ. Their hearts were never changed by the Holy Spirit so that on hearing the Good News they could believe it and cast their hope of salvation on Jesus. They remained in unrepentant rebellion against God. This Great White Throne Judgment is for them.

The **Bema** *Seat Judgment*

The other judgment is for the Believer, and it's called the *Bema*

Chapter 6: Investing in Our Eternity

Judgment, occurring before the *Bema* Seat Judgment. (2 Tim 4:8) This judgment addresses what you, by faith, have allowed the Holy Spirit to do through your life. (1 Cor 3:12-4:5) This judgment is not talked about much in our generation, but before this Seat you will receive God's reward for your works on earth before entering heaven. (Matt 5:12; 6:19-21; Rev 3:5, 10, 21)

Bema is an ancient Greek word.[1] Although at the time of Christ it could describe: a tribunal seat, a judicial bench, a judgment seat, or the throne of the one in charge, the use appropriated to the New Testament's description is the physical arrangement of the award ceremony following a sporting event. The Expanded Bible names it in an inline comment on 2 Corinthians, Chapter 5, verse 10.[2]

So, as used in this Biblical metaphor, the *Bema* is:
- *the seat* of judgment upon which the event judge sits to follow every action of the competitor.
- *the purpose* of the judgment to determine the result and to assign the reward for the competitor.
- *the stand* upon which the competitor receives the "judgment, *or* **reward**" assigned to the competitor. And, yes, it's even that same, literal, tiered, Olympic presentation stand we have all seen on television at the Olympic Games!

The *seat*, *purpose* of the judgment, reward presentation *stand*, and the term, are carryovers from the original Greek Olympic and Istemal games begun before the time of Christ. See **Figure 6-1. The Bema – Olympic Seat and Stand**. The New Testament's metaphoric descriptions of this "judgment" event survive today in our own culture through the use of the *stand* and its *purpose* to hand out rewards. You can see it in the modern Olympic games as the athletes take their positions to receive their gold, silver, or bronze medal.

Figure 6-1

---

1 https://www.merriam-webster.com/dictionary/bema. See its description at: https://bible.org/article/doctrine-rewards-judgment-seat-bema-christ
2 The Expanded Bible, Thomas Nelson Inc. Nashville. 2011.

> **"NOW, THE ETERNAL REWARDS WE RECEIVE AT THE *BEMA* JUDGMENT SEAT ARE BASED ON WHAT YOU, AS A CONDUIT OF THE HOLY SPIRIT, HAVE ALLOWED HIM TO DO WITH, AND THROUGH YOU."**

Now, the eternal rewards we receive at the *Bema* Seat Judgment are based on what you, as a conduit of the Holy Spirit, have allowed Him to do with, and through you. (1 Cor 3:12-4:5)

It goes back to stewardship, ownership, and allowing the Holy Spirit, by faith, to direct the time, talent, treasure, understanding, and relationships that God gives you, and over which He has also given you stewardship authority (Matt 25:14-30) to use them to His glory. Remember, these are His anyway. (Psa 50:7-15)

So, when He directs you in your stewardship, it's much better for you to comply than to mistakenly think that your wealth is yours to do with as you wish. You can also "lose" (or not receive) reward (1 Cor 3:15) by not attending to His direction or leading. You can ultimately suffer the loss of those rewards (1 Cor 3:15-17; Heb 4:11-13) God had otherwise intended for you, as I've already illustrated from my own life.

The Eternal Rewards of a Christian Life

The New Testament is full of references to rewards for the believer (look them up!):
- Jesus promises great rewards for faithful service, (Rev 11:18)
- Loyal servants are rewarded for works done in this life by faith, (1 Cor 4:5)
- Committed believers who leave everything behind are generously rewarded – a hundred times over for their personal investment in His spiritual kingdom, here on earth. (Matt 19:29)

There are rewards for,
- Denying ourselves, (Matt 16:24-27)
- Being compassionate towards the needy, (Luke 14:13-14)
- Showing kindness to our enemies, (Luke 6:35)
- Giving generously, (Matt 19:21)

- Providing hospitality and preparing a meal for the poor, (Luke 14:14)
- Living a life of Godliness.

There is also a great reward for,
- trusting God through difficult circumstances, (Heb 10:34-36)
- persevering through persecution for the sake of Jesus Christ. (Luke 6:22-23)

What could those heavenly rewards possibly be? No one knows for sure, but I know these rewards will be a far greater blessing than we can now even imagine or comprehend. They have an eternal significance and are everlasting. (Rev 3:5, 10, 21, 22; 22:12) There are several "Crowns" (rewards) mentioned in the New Testament for the believer:

- The Crown of Righteousness: This crown is given for joyfully being ready to meet Christ at His return. (2 Tim 4:6-8)
- The Crown of Glory: A reward given for faithfully serving Christ in a position of leadership. (1 Pet 5:1-4)
- The Crown of Life: Given for trusting Christ in persecution (James 1:12, Rev 2:10)
- The Incorruptible Crown: Victory and Discipline earns this reward from our Heavenly Father. (1 Cor 9:24-25)
- The Crown of Rejoicing: Given for serving others with a life of discipleship. (1 Thes 2:15, Phil 4:1)

There is also yet another kind of reward referred to in the New Testament—a reward of authority or rule in His kingdom.

According to Revelation 20:6, its recipients will reign with Christ, and be put in charge of many things. (Matt 25:21-23) Some followers through their service to Jesus will be given rule over cities in proportion to their faithfulness, one given 11 cities, another five cities, and yet another, none at all. (Luke 19:21-24) Paul notes that "we" will judge the world—and even judge angels (1 Cor 6:2-3) which is honestly hard to wrap my head around.

It becomes clear from these passages that all Christians will be with Christ, (1 Cor 3:15) but only some will be given authority. (Rev 3:21) Only some will reign with Jesus. (2 Tim 2:12)

It is here, within these verses, that I got my illustration of the

Olympic games. Imagine we are there at the opening ceremony, and it is Jesus on the main stage at the *Bema*. The light is His radiant glory (Rev 21:23-25; John 8:12) shining brighter than the noon-day sun. The excitement and overwhelming joy of just being there, at the Judgment Seat of Christ, (Rom 14:17) is unspeakable, watching others receive their rewards, (2 Cor 5:10) awaiting your turn and your time to share in the pure and holy consuming presence of Jesus. (Rev 4:8) He is about to take His time with you, meticulously going over every worthy thought, deed, action and sacrifice of your life, discussing them, considering each (2 Cor 5:10) for its value, its measure in eternal significance, and suddenly you begin to feel the Father, Son and Holy Spirit. (2 Cor 13:4) It's palpable. You can literally taste and see the Lord is good. (Psa 25:8; 34:8) As you approach closer and closer to the *Bema*, His Holy light intensifies, (Rev 21:23-25; John 8:12) and it wraps around you, warming you, while the overwhelming joy of the Lord intensifies, as you ponder this event. He is ready to recount what you, by faith, allowed the Holy Spirit to do through your life. (Heb 4:11-13)

Then it happens: Jesus' loving eyes (John 15:16-17) lock deep into your soul. You have never been so fearfully yet trustingly been laid bare, as the One who created you reveals your 1ife, (1 Pet 1:5; Heb 9:27; Heb 4:11-13) your earthly significance, and as it now impacts your standing for eternity. (2 Cor 5:10) Jesus begins looking back at how your life affected the world around you in ways you could not fathom for good and eternal reward. (Gal 6:7-8) For some, Jesus concludes by saying; "For you, my son or daughter, I reward you the Crown of Rejoicing, (Gal 6:7-8) for the love you demonstrated in sharing the Good News

> **JESUS BEGINS LOOKING BACK AT HOW YOUR LIFE AFFECTED THE WORLD AROUND YOU IN WAYS YOU COULD NOT FATHOM FOR GOOD AND ETERNAL REWARD.**

with those I sent to you and the Crown of Righteousness (2Tim 4:8) for your years of faithfulness as you kept pure, as the Holy Spirit revealed His sanctifying power in your life. I also reward you the Incorruptible Crown (1 Cor 9:24-27) for your determination to overcome the battles in your life and the victories you received."

Then, imagine Jesus wrapping His arms around you and saying,

"Well done, good and faithful servant." (Luke 19:11-27; Matt 25:14-30) At that moment, two angels (Matt 18:10) swoop down to your side and usher you to your seat, just three rows back from the *Bema*. As you are seated, there is great applause and cheers of joy. You dare to glance at the two angels. Their faces are beaming with joy as smiles stretch across their faces. They look vaguely familiar to you, but you're not sure. As you settle into your seat, they speedily fly back to the immense crowd of angels over the stage. (Acts 1:9-11) It's like a bright cloud. They are all singing and worshiping the Lord (Heb 1:4-14) as He is yet hugging another believer, after receiving their rewards. You glance back up, and now you cannot see your two escorts. They have blended into what seem to be millions of angels overhead. You also realize that two different angels are escorting the person now leaving the *Bema*. Those angels have the same look of joy and loving pride on their faces. The person next to you leans over and whispers, "Those are our guardian angels. (Matt 18:10) They have been with us our whole earthly life. They too have been waiting for this day!" (2 Tim 4:8; 1 Cor 4:5)

You celebrate with the others for the remainder of the day, as one after another receives their rewards. You can't help but notice that some are escorted straight to Jesus' throne, (Rom 8:34) but others to the rows in front of you, still within the glorious light that spills out from the *Bema* Seat. But, most by far, are led past you and into what seems like darkness behind you. (Rev 21:23-26; John 8:12) As you stare out into that darkness you realize that it's not pitch black, it only seems to be, compared to the light surrounding you from the Throne. The light dissipates the further each one gets from the *Bema* and Christ.

As you look back to Jesus, your heart just longs to be next to Him again, (Luke 15:20) in the full presence of His light, (Rev 21:23-26; John 8:12) and in His arms. (Luke 15:20) You are over-joyed to have received three crowns; (Matt 16:27) but, there is a longing to have received the other two, and more, because, that would have placed you on His throne and in His full presence forever. (Rev 2:7, 10-11; 3:10-12) Not all of us will have authority. (Luke 19:17-26) We'll all actually have differing rewards. (1 Cor 3:12-15)

My friend, this is hard to write, but not all Christians will receive treasure in heaven (Matt 6:1-4 and 19-21) or rewards. Sadly, Scripture suggests that some Christians, that is, those who do not "abide in Him" (KJV) or "continue in Him" (NIV), will be "ashamed" of what commands they did or didn't follow either because of inattentiveness or lack of a "surrendered life" commitment to Christ at His coming. (1 John 2:28) Although it seems hard to understand that some regret will continue in heaven, nevertheless we must realize and take away from the *Bema* Seat illustration this one idea. It will matter; it will matter *significantly* – because all of our eternity will be impacted by our faithfulness to Jesus' commands, and yielding to the Holy Spirit's leading during our earthly lives.

In other words, our earthly lives are a guaranteed investment into eternity, just as Jesus advises us all in Matthew 6:19-20 and even more for those who have a higher calling and responsibility to His flock in Matthew 13:52.

My imperfect, yet hopefully, insightful Olympic illustration of the *Bema* Seat Judgment helps me, and I hope you too, to get a sense of the importance of our rewards. Like the Olympic athletes or the audience, you will be glad, just to be there. I can't help but think that you'll long to have been in the full presence of the glory of the Lord and to serve and reign with Him for all of eternity.

> **"I CAN'T HELP BUT THINK THAT YOU'LL LONG TO HAVE BEEN IN THE FULL PRESENCE OF THE GLORY OF THE LORD AND TO SERVE AND REIGN WITH HIM FOR ALL OF ETERNITY."**

No matter how we attempt to describe The *Bema* Seat Judgment, or imperfectly explain it, the fact remains that each of us will have differing eternal experiences, (Rom 2:5-6) rewards, and positions. (1 Cor 3:10; Rev 2:7; 10-11, 3:10-12) These eternal experiences are being cast through our faithfulness to the Master in this earthly life. (Rev 2:7, 10-11; 3-10-12, 19-22) This life that we have been generously given provides an opportunity – a once in a lifetime window – to determine how our *Bema* Seat Judgment will unfold, whether for reward or not. (1 Cor 6:13-15) It all hinges on what you - by faith - choose to allow the Holy Spirit to do through your life now. (Heb 4:11-13; 2 Tim 3:14-17; John 14:26)

The Significance of The Gift

It was late in the afternoon when my wife called the private line into my office.

Chapter 6: Investing in Our Eternity

"It's gone, all gone," she sobbed.

"What's gone?'" I replied.

"All of it, everything, everything in the house is gone!" she pressed.

"I don't understand. Slow down and explain." I requested.

My wife arrived home that spring afternoon, with a car full of groceries and kids, only to walk through the front door to find all of our furniture, electronics, and some memorabilia gone. Our 1,800 square foot rented house was cleaned out. Everything was gone except our clothes, the beds, and some dishes. Some personal items, photos, and boxes in the garage were left or neatly stacked on the floor. The house was almost exactly like the day we moved in, without the moving trucks outside. I packed up my things at the office and numbly headed home, stopping only to pick up a pizza, since we had no cooking utensils to make dinner. That night, after all the commotion as a family, we sat down together in a circle on the dining room floor and laughed about the situation, ate pizza, and prayed together.

My youngest son asked, with concern beyond his years, "Papa, what are we going to sit on tomorrow?"

"I'm not sure, but I do know God will provide," (Matt 6:30) I responded, hoping to reassure him.

That night, as my wife and I lay in bed, we again took our needs before God in prayer. We were a young family with not much savings and no renter's insurance. It's not like we had any tangible things of true value. Most items were hand-me-downs, not worth much, plus a few family heirlooms. It was the inconvenience that was the hardest for the whole family to cope with. My wife had always tried to make a comfortable home and has never cared if we had fancy things. As long as they were practical, it was enough. This really pushed her out of her comfort zone. The situation wasn't practical and certainly not homey.

By the next morning, the word had gotten out about our situation. By mid-morning, the kids were at school and Kim and I were at the office when a call came in. It was my friend Patrick, a local businessman with whom I attended a men's Bible study.

"Good morning, Pat. How are you?" I answered his call.

"Good morning, Mike. My wife and I heard about your situation, and we want to help."

"Pat, that is very nice, but I am sure it will work itself out in time," I replied.

"Look, you need furniture, right? Furniture I have. And I want to help, so this seems like the answer to the prayers you've been praying – you have been praying, haven't you?" Pat firmly responded.

"Well, sure, we've been praying. But I don't want to put you out, I mean ...."

Pat cut me off; "Mike, you and Kim come over to my store at, say, 4:00 pm, and we'll see what we can do. Ok?"

"Ok," I responded hesitantly, not really sure what he meant.

"Good! See you then." And click, his call was over.

I rushed into Kim's office to report the phone conversation. Neither of us were sure what to think. My friend Pat owned a large furniture showroom in town. Later that afternoon, around 3:30, we jumped into the car and headed to the bank. We pulled out all the cash we dared, $1,100.00, and headed to our 4 pm meeting with Pat at his furniture showroom. As we entered his office, he welcomed us.

We sat across from him, and he opened with, "Okay, so what do you need?"

"Well, we need everything," I explained. Then, I detailed what was left, leading to; "We only need a few things to get us by. We have eleven hundred dollars." As I placed the cash on his desk, he smiled.

"Mike, I'd rather you kept your cash for things I don't carry, you know, pots, pans, electronics ... stuff like that," as he pushed the money back across the desk towards me. "I think you're misunderstanding me. I want you to go out into the showroom and pick out your house."

Stunned silence was all we could offer. He grabbed the phone on his desk and paged his General Manager. Within a few minutes, his manager walked in.

"John, these are the Sticklers, Mike and Kim." As we shook hands, he continued, "Please take them into the showroom and help them pick out their house, whatever they want, as long as it's on-hand, in inventory. We'll need to deliver it in the morning. Once you complete the order form, check the inventory, and have the guys load up the trucks and bring me the invoice. I'll take it from there."

"Ok," John replied. "Mr. and Mrs. Stickler, will you please follow me?"

We hugged Pat, with tears in our eyes, still not really sure what this all meant – with a whisper of, "Thank you!"

For the next few hours, we walked throughout the showroom floor, selecting each room of the house, the living room, dining room, den, office, and each bedroom. We changed our minds about the style and overall decor at least twice. We sat on chairs, laid down on couches, and tried out lamps. The only way I can describe the experience is if you ever watched one of those TV shows, where a sweepstakes winner gets just so many minutes to fill as many shopping carts as he can. The difference here being, we had no time limit.

At first, Kim was shopping by price, what was on sale, *etc*. Then John stopped us. "Pat wants to bless you. Please make your decisions by the tastes and styles you want. You have not been given a budget." Even with that directive, Kim was reluctant, not wanting to take advantage of Pat's generosity. After a bit more redirection and prompting by the General Manager, her reluctance waned and then it really got to be fun. She got to fulfill a dream that I think most of us would have. The dream of a free shopping spree!

The next morning, Pat's trucks arrived bright and early. My boys were overjoyed as each piece of furniture was unloaded and unwrapped. Within just a couple of hours, and for the first time ever, we had a house full of brand-new furniture. So much so, that we needed to send one item back. We just didn't have room for it. Not long after the trucks were unloaded, Pat showed up at the front door. I hadn't seen him since we left his office the day before. He took about an hour to show us all the features of our new furniture. We shared some laughs as our boys ran from one piece of furniture to the next trying each one out, then making claims of which was their personal favorite and which chair they called "dibs" on. But, with all my family's excitement, I couldn't help but notice the joy Pat felt—along with his smile and laughter. I *know* he was having a better time than all of us put together! His extraordinary generosity to us seemed to be an even bigger blessing to him than it was for us. And trust me, it was a BIG blessing to us!

That single day changed my life forever. It became the foundation for how we decided to live our lives even to this day. We decided that we wanted to live our lives in such a way that we would be a blessing to others in every way God would show us. (Rom 15:1-7)

LIFE WITHOUT RESERVATION

We wanted to live like my friend Pat, passing along God's resources, as He would direct us, without reservation. (2 Cor 9:6-15) That one gift became a significant turning point for us to live a generous life and a life without reservation. It's hard to believe, but that was over twenty years ago. Who knew where it would take me? Apparently, God did!

Today, I spend my days studying and telling stories of generous lives lived. There has been a progression, a road of sorts, that has gotten me here.

At the beginning of this journey, my first calling was into the ministry – and my pastor suggested I help a local homeless mission, as they needed a lay pastor. I met with their Founder and Executive Director, and after several meetings, we agreed on a start date. On that first Sunday, I was to preach to the homeless. That morning came, but the founder didn't. Not only was he absent, but he also didn't tell anyone I was coming. So, we waited, as the people all assembled, and after about an hour the assistant director walked up to me and said, "I don't know where he is, but if you have something to say, share it." So, I did. It seemed to go okay, and honestly, I don't even remember what I said.

Later that night, about dinnertime, I got a call from the Executive Director. He was angry. He claimed that he never agreed to have me serve as lay pastor, that I was not welcome at the mission again. I was confused. I reminded him that we met together several times and even signed an agreement – a job contract of sorts – even though there was no pay or remuneration involved. He stuttered at this information as if he didn't remember any of it, then reaffirmed to me to not come back to the mission. As I hung up the phone, I was perplexed at what just happened. I was sure this was the place God wanted me to serve, so I hit my knees in prayer. After a few minutes in deep, yet confused, prayer, I felt like all I heard was GO! I came out of my office and into the kitchen where Kim was preparing dinner. I related the story of what had just happened. I told her I wasn't sure of what to do. She listened quietly, then without missing a beat said; "If you're sure this is what God wants you to do … GO!"

> **"IF YOU'RE SURE THIS IS WHAT GOD WANTS YOU TO DO ... GO!"**

The next Sunday, I was there, ready to share a message. The Executive Director did not show again. The Assistant Director invited me up as before. The following Sunday, I showed up, and the founder didn't. I shared a message again. The next week it happened again, and so on. During the weekdays, I would stop in at the mission and help where I could. Soon, I was building relationships with the residents and staff.

After eight months of just helping where I could and serving on Sundays, I was invited to a board meeting. It turned out I was the last person to talk with the founder and Executive Director. He had disappeared, apparently off the face of the earth, and even his wife and children didn't know his whereabouts. The board had called me in to offer me his job. In time, I accepted, and thus began a journey I never expected.

As it turns out, the Executive Director had suffered a complete mental breakdown. He was picked up by the police, detained, and taken to the mental health hospital, where he stayed until he stabilized months later. Even though his family frantically searched for him, by law, the mental health hospital could not affirm or deny he was there. Unfortunately, he had struggled for years with his mental health.

During my tenure at the mission, I began to learn the depths of God's mercy and grace.

I also learned the differences between fundraising and sales. I had up until that point been involved in sales techniques, and when I tried to apply those processes to fundraising, the attempts failed.

But once I discovered how to switch to fundraising, we as a mission became much more successful in our endeavors. But, most importantly, the Holy Spirit began to mature my skills as a shepherd, (Col 1:9-12) as well as my love for people (Col 3:12-14) and the art of listening.

After the mission years, I pastored at a local church plant and then began a business that aided ministries in their fundraising techniques. Eventually, I built a business and reputation that attracted some of the most notable ministries and churches in the world. We had three offices and 25 employees.

And I hated it.

Inwardly, God was dealing with me, showing me that the fundraising approach and techniques I had learned ... and developed ... and taught, even as different as they were from sales, are not His way. His church doesn't need more money. It needed to experience generosity (2 Cor 9:6-15) and to *be* generous. He showed and *clarified* for me the acts of generosity I had seen over the years. A generosity that was initiated out of responsibility for being a steward of the Master's relationships, talents, money, and understanding of the Master's time.

Generosity is much more than giving money. It's a way of life, living in response to a generous God. I began to study, pray for clarification and understanding and ask those I knew around me who lived generously for insight. In time, I began to see that my business as a whole was not really in alignment with the heart of God and that there was a better way, a more Biblical way.

> **"GENEROSITY IS MUCH MORE THAN GIVING MONEY. IT'S A WAY OF LIFE, LIVING IN RESPONSE TO A GENEROUS GOD."**

I became convinced I needed to make changes, stop the fundraising consulting, and start teaching about generosity and a life without reservation.

Oh, it would be messy. I had clients and staff who depended on my old methodology. It was a system that had been used for generations by the church and one that (to be honest) was used by the world and had been adopted by God's people. I slowly began to change how I was doing things, affectionately referring to myself as a "recovering fundraiser;" but apparently my growth in understanding was going too slowly for God and so right at that point came the Haiti debacle. The change came much faster from that point on, and although I was able to embrace it, the challenge was keeping up!

Chapter 7
LIVING A LIFE WITHOUT RESERVATION

A life without reservation is first and foremost a life of grace. (Eph 2:4-10) A life that is ever mindful of God's extravagant grace towards us, (Eph 1:1-14) through His Son. It's His grace that is manifest through us for others, in any given situation. It's giving with the Love turned up to high. (2 Cor 9:6) Along with my last-chapter about my Bible-study friend, Patrick, let me share some examples of others I know who live generously.

GENEROSITY IN BUSINESS

My friend, Norm Miller, is a great Christian leader who demonstrates a life without reservation. Being from Texas, he has a simple motto when you ask him for his secret to a life without reservation. He says: "I keep my eyes open and my ear to the ground."

Norm is the chairman of Interstate Batteries, as well as an astute and successful business leader. He also lives with one passion: "What does God want me to do with the success He has given me?"

He told me:

> "It's simple. I keep my eyes open for what God is doing through the lives around me and in the lives He puts in my path. Then, I prayerfully investigate the substance of what He sees."

Norm does this often with a staff of people – he employs some chaplains whose primary purpose is to investigate opportunities that are then presented to him. Norm "keeps his ears to the ground," as well, by listening to others around him who lead lives without reservation and who may be supporting organizations or people who have a vision similar to his.

And Norm likes to get his hands dirty – often traveling right into the mission field. Wherever the Lord leads him, he follows. A faithful steward of his Master's resources, Norm is willing to direct all he manages for the Lord to where his Master desires, including relationships. Norm is always gracious, polite, and responsive – to every email or call.

Given a great deal of Kingdom resources to manage, he has no ego to protect and no image to uphold. Love and kindness are his hallmarks. Compassion his trademark. His life, without reservation.

GENEROSITY IN THE CHURCH

Along the eastern side of the Sierra Nevada Mountains in Northern Nevada, is a little church that has faithfully loved the people in their community for nearly 20 plus years. Calvary Chapel of Carson City is a small community of believers who have a generous impact on this high desert town that is Nevada's State Capital. It's pastor, Pat Propster, has an infectious smile and laugh, both of which impart the love of God to whomever he encounters.

Pastor Pat is the kind of man who finds it almost impossible to simply *shop* at the local Home Depot because he knows everyone. They are all his friends – and they each want to talk to him. What might take you or me ten minutes to buy, will often take Pastor Pat 45 minutes because he stops to love on everyone he meets.

It's Pat Propster to whom the state assemblymen and Governor come for advice during difficult legislative sessions. And, it's Calvary Chapel that is sought out for prominent funeral ceremonies, weddings, and such.

Pastor Pat's infectious and caring approach has rubbed off into the congregation of this Calvary Chapel. They are usually the first on the scene when one of Carson's families or the City's community has a need, sacrificially giving of the time, talent, treasure, understanding, and their relationships which God has entrusted to them to meet that need. This is a church, who, like its leader, is spiritual, vibrant, and healthy. It lives its love affair with a generous God in a lifestyle without reservation.

> **"IT LIVES ITS LOVE AFFAIR WITH A GENEROUS GOD IN A LIFESTYLE WITHOUT RESERVATION."**

Chapter 7: Living a Life Without Reservation

GENEROSITY WITH THE UNDERSTANDING GOD HAS GIVEN

A few years ago, I was watching a TV program about the so-called, "Hanoi Hilton," the notorious prison in Vietnam where many of our soldiers experienced horrific treatment while prisoners of war. One of the interviewees was Guy Gruters, a prisoner held there for over five years during which he was tortured almost daily. As I watched the program, I felt there must be something different about this man. They had interviewed several men, but Mr. Gruters had a peace about him. I wondered if he was a Christian. So, I had my producer contact him and inquire if he would be an appropriate guest for our radio program.

As it turned out, he was (and still is) a Christian and had been for a long time. While on our program, he told a mind-blowing story of hate and forgiveness. He recalled how each day the North Vietnamese guards would tie his hands behind his back and then hoist him in the air from the wrists. While he swung under his own weight, in terrible pain, they would beat him, interrogate him, and then beat him again. At the end of the torture session they would lock him in a cage that was so small he could not stand up – only kneel. There, while in the forced kneeling position, he would pray for God to forgive his torturers.

His description was startlingly vivid, even 50 years later. I asked, "How did you get to a place of forgiveness that enabled you to pray for these inhuman, evil people?" His response shaped my life and understanding about forgiveness;

"I DIDN'T REALLY FORGIVE THEM ... ESPECIALLY WHILE THEY TORTURED ME."

"Mike, at first, I didn't mean it ... I didn't really forgive them ... especially while they tortured me. I'd remembered Matthew 5:44, 'But I say to you, love your enemies, pray for those who persecute you,' and so, I did it just out of obedience to the Lord. But, in time – over about six months – my heart began to change, and I really did forgive them, even as the torture continued. In time, I could actually tell them I loved them."

Today, after all these years later, Guy speaks around the world and writes about forgiveness. He generously shares the understanding God has given him about true forgiveness and his finally-internalized understanding of Matthew 5:44. And because of this understanding of his generous God, Guy's life centers on forgiveness without reservation.

GENEROSITY FROM HOME

Then there's my friend Kathy. Kathy has a quick wit, infectious smile, and a joy that lights up a room. Kathy has had some tough times. She and her husband, not able to have biological children, adopted a beautiful girl who became the light of their life. Over the years, their daughter became interested in competitive figure skating. They sacrificed everything to get the best coaches and training they could afford. Their daughter became moderately successful as she competed around the country. Again, all at great sacrifice to her parents.

Then, the first sadness hit this family. As their daughter finished high school and became a young adult, she became disappointed in the life she was given by the only parents she ever knew and ceased all contact with them. Then, Kathy experienced multiple health problems. Shortly after, when Kathy needed her husband most, he died suddenly, leaving her disabled and alone.

That's when she met Jesus for the first time and accepted His mercy and grace. She has never looked back on her life as a series of disappointments. Though she is still physically disabled, she lives her life unto the Lord.

She can't drive, but every time her church is open, she's there to volunteer as a church greeter, help serve, and be an inspiration to others. She loves to use her cell phone to call others and encourage them. She keeps her nose in the Bible and studies it to increase her understanding.

And she prays.

And prays.

Working through her disability, she sends encouraging greeting cards to everyone; prisoners, shut-ins, church members, or anyone to whom she believes the Holy Spirit has led her.

All I know is when I meet a person like Kathy, I wonder just how many crowns she will have in heaven. Undoubtedly more than I. Despite all that has limited her physically, relationally, and emotionally, Kathy lives her life for those in her life without reservation.

> **"I WONDER HOW MANY CROWNS SHE WILL HAVE IN HEAVEN."**

GENEROSITY IN HARD CIRCUMSTANCES

Another person I am honored to call a friend is Jerry Brewer. Here is a man in federal prison – more than halfway through serving a 15-year sentence for a white-collar crime; but, one of the most giving people I have ever met. Though he doesn't have many material resources, he always attends to everyone's needs.

He is a super intelligent guy – with an MBA (which is not as rare as you might think in prison). Though he's old enough to collect social security, he's very fit, and can give men thirty years his junior a run for their money while playing soccer. He uses his intelligence, education, and fitness to help the men where he is incarcerated by teaching classes, writing and typing legal briefs, and using sports to make and maintain relationships. He shares his understanding through leading Bible studies, discipleship, and providing leadership to the prison church.

He befriends the friendless and is the only guy I know who will give you the dessert right off his meal tray, which in prison is the equivalent of giving someone your wedding ring right off your finger. Why would he do this? Because he figures you can use it more than he can, plus he just wants to bless you.

In the short few years I have known him, each day he would greet me with, "Do you need anything?" This is extraordinary if you think about it. There we were, supposedly in the one place on all the earth that everyone thinks of himself first, and Jerry is first thinking of others.

He truly considers all others greater than himself, as in Philemon 2:3:

> *Do nothing out of selfish ambition or vain conceit.*
> *Rather, in humility, value others above yourselves*

Jerry is a man who gives without reservation – even to his own needs.

GENEROSITY WITH RELATIONSHIPS

Peter Strople has been named the most connected man in America. It's true. His "friends of Peter" contact list is impressive, but it's more than a list of names and numbers. These are people with whom Peter has lovingly cultivated deep relationships. Think of the Fortune 500 CEOs, celebrities, ministry leaders, presidents, and industry thought-leaders. It seems Peter knows them all, or if he doesn't, he knows someone who does and will introduce them to each other.

Now, you would think that he has cultivated these relationships to use for his business or to sell them something. But no, he doesn't keep them close to his vest. In fact, he cultivates these relationships specifically to share them with others who could use the contact in developing and maintaining their personal and professional lives' needs.

This is how he does it:

Once he gets to know you, he will ask you a question like "Name five people who can change the way you do business, or who can take you to the next level." After a few minutes of coaxing you through your list, he then pulls out his cell phone, puts it on speaker, and calls them. No matter who they are, they always seem to take his call. Then, he starts the call with something like this: "It's Peter Strople, I have my friend, Mike Stickler, here with me. He's an amazing author who wants to get his books in Walmart" (just an example). At the conclusion of the call, he asks, "Can Mike call you directly if he has other questions? May I give him your direct line?"

For Peter, they always seem to say "Yes!" … and, "Yes!"

I have learned from Peter that relationships are more valuable than money, reputation, or just about anything else. When you are Peter's friend, you have entered into a wonderful club, of sorts, one that opens up a whole new world of people you may never before have dreamed of knowing. People who are not afraid to share with you whatever they have if it will bless you or fill your need, somehow.

Once you become a "friend of Peter," your friends become his friends and vice-versa. It's not some weird artificial network; rather, it's just a very natural, organic, un-stated thing ... of which you definitely want to be part.

Peter's life has taught me a great deal about how relationships matter. They need cultivation, nurturing, shepherding, stewardship, and exercise! Peter lovingly exercises (shares) the rich relationships God has given him – without reservation.

> **"PETER'S LIFE HAS TAUGHT ME A GREAT DEAL ABOUT HOW RELATIONSHIPS MATTER. THEY NEED CULTIVATION, NURTURING, SHEPHERDING, STEWARDSHIP, AND EXERCISE!"**

GENEROSITY – ENVISIONED AND ORGANIZED FOR OTHERS' BENEFIT

Generosity can and should be practiced by all. As a parent, these principles should be taught and instilled in our children. If we can help our children develop the Biblical practice of stewardship and considering all others to be greater than ourselves, we will be giving them and the world a great legacy.

Yasha Gupta, the founder of Sight Learning (sightlearning.com), is an excellent example of a young man with a simple vision (no pun intended) leading a life without reservation. He is someone who saw a need and simply thought he could help provide the means for others to fulfill it.

Yasha had grown up wearing eyeglasses. His glasses were something he took for granted and had never experienced a time in his life without this necessary aid. Then one day, as a young student, he lost them. For one week his glasses were gone and he then discovered just how indispensable they were to him and how difficult life is when you can't see clearly. This caused Yasha to think; 'What if I had never received this indispensable tool for my life? How do children learn to read without eyeglasses? How do they identify the landscape, their house or their parents? How do they cope?'

This one experience changed Yasha's life. He began to think and come up with ways he could get the thousands of pairs of eyeglasses that were discarded here in the United States into the hands of children around the world. By helping those who otherwise had no access to them, he could enable them to see clearly for the first time in their lives – and from then, on! The implications of this small effort would have an immeasurable impact on the lives of people he didn't know. Maybe one of these children who could now see would learn to read and go to college. Maybe become a doctor, engineer, or teacher. This one small act on his part could undoubtedly change lives for the better. How could he not try?

Yasha began collecting discarded eyeglasses from friends, families, local eyeglass stores, community groups, and whomever he could in order to stockpile enough to meet the demand. But, just collecting used glasses was only the start. Those eyeglasses would need to be tested, examined for their prescription strength, and then matched to a child with the need for its prescription strength in that eye, or both, in order to meet the child's exactly needed eye correction.

This would be a significant obstacle for one young and generous heart. So, Yasha paired up with non-profits and non-governmental organizations who could help with the matching and completing the process to fulfill his vision of helping children get eyeglasses. Today, Yasha is a college student at the University of Southern California, Los Angeles. He continues with his work, making a difference through his organization Sight Learning, while his generous heart continues to grow, always seeking how he can help to make a difference ... without reservation.

GENEROUS TO THE ENVIRONMENT

Somehow, public stewardship of the environment has been abdicated by humanity to the world governments whose predominant worldview is simply not appropriate to its management. But over the past few years, I have seen Christians re-assert both the Biblical understanding of Creation, *i.e.,* "the earth and everything in it," – a phrase of both the Old Testament (Psa 24:1) and the New Testament (1Cor 10: 26) – and their role as the Master's stewards of it (Gen 2:15 and Luke 12:42-44).

Steve Fitch is just such a man. Dr. Fitch was a pastor and long-time denominational executive who began to rethink Christian world missions in a whole new and holistic way. Steve grew up as an

"MK" (*missionary's kid*) and has seen and experienced the effectiveness of the modern church and its effort to bring aid to populations around the world who seem to have real difficulty feeding themselves. Using his lifetime of experience and by simply taking a step back from the mission field, he began developing a vision that has real merit.

In Ethiopia, the people living in proximity to Lake Awasa continually experienced potential starvation. They didn't realize that cutting down all of the trees in the adjacent Rift Valley's forest would have severe consequences. Over the years, millions of trees had been cut down for cooking, heating and building needs until, finally, the Rift Valley's forests became barren. Massive erosion followed from increasing amounts of rain run-offs and led to flooding (which had never existed before) during the annual rainy season.

One year, I went with Steve to Lake Awasa and heard the stories from the village elders about how there used to be herds of antelope, kudu, and elephants. Now the herds were gone. The bigger concern was the cycle of drought that parched the land and flooding that eroded it when it finally did rain. They had only a few wells and those began to dry up, too – because, without the forest trees to hold the rain as it fell, the water table began to drop with the rainwater running off into the lake instead of percolating into the soil and refilling the ancient aquifers.

Of course, without water, there were no crops, no animals to hunt, and no wood to burn. Instead, each day, the women, children, and livestock would make the 14-mile round-trip trek to the lake to fill every water container they could lay their hands on just to stay alive. Their situation was desperate. Although they lived in an area that was helped by Christian ministries, hundreds of these people were at risk of relocation from their ancestral lands into some type of government-run refugee camp. They would be moved far away from their homeland, and their children would be put into government-run schools. It would take generations to overcome such a move.

After much prayer, Steve began putting his vision into action. He persuaded the Ethiopian Government to allow him to use a few acres along the lake shore to build a tree nursery to grow acacia trees from seed. Under the supervision of the nursery manager, twice a day, dozens of local families would descend upon the nursery to hand-water each seedling. While I was there, I asked Steve, "Why do they water in such an inefficient fashion?" (I had studied and grown up in agriculture and knew there were many other ways to irrigate that would be far more effective.)

His answer surprised me:

"Mike, by hand-watering each plant, several goals get accomplished at the same time.

First, the small amount of pay those people receive, about one dollar per day, impacts the economy of the entire village, and basically, it's cheaper than the 'more-efficient' infrastructure, too.

The second reason is that the husbandry the locals provide gets them to buy-in to sustaining this project. But most importantly, our manager uses each day to teach the entire community one-by-one, how this process will benefit them, ensuring their safety from the ever-looming potential of being displaced."

His thinking was brilliant!

Steve's efforts were even more thorough and thoughtful as he used the locals to transplant the trees into their permanent home as they began restoring the Rift Valley. He then hired a roving guard, of sorts, to protect the saplings from grazing animals until they reached maturity and he taught the elders why this effort was so pivotal and important to their environmental needs. He also educated the locals about growing other trees on their own plots of land, such as those useful for food and wood. By doing so, they would prevent the developing permanent forest in the Rift Valley from being once again cut down, resulting again in deforestation and the environmental horror it brings.

This one man, raising a few thousand dollars and using his experience and education, saved an entire group of people. It's been over ten years since I traveled to Ethiopia to see the Eden Project, as it is known today, but I enjoy visiting their

> **"THIS ONE MAN, RAISING A FEW THOUSAND DOLLARS AND USING HIS EXPERIENCE AND EDUCATION, SAVED AN ENTIRE GROUP OF PEOPLE."**

website and seeing the progress they have made. The trees (some which I personally helped to plant), are now fully grown into a maturing perma-forest, and the locals are still living on their homeland. They are thriving, all because of Steve's vision to live his life to give life without reservation.

I have given you examples of eight generous lives. You can now see that from wherever you start, the flame from God that burns within can produce such a life without reservation!

It Always Seems to be About MONEY

I hope you noticed I didn't focus on money. That's where most authors, speakers, and consultants start when writing or teaching about generosity. There is a thought out there that 'generosity' is all about the people's need to give more money.

There are volumes of studies that demonstrate that financial giving is pitifully small. This information is then presented in such a way as to make you feel guilty, but, since you don't want to feel guilty, *you will automatically give more.*

Another thought is that if you could just *see* the "need," the hungry children, the homeless, the sick and neglected animals, then you'll feel bad, but since you don't want to feel bad, you *will quickly* give *more.*

A different popular mantra says that if you give more, then God will make you rich, or *richer*, because if you're not rich then you should feel bad but, since you don't want to feel bad, so you *must* give more.

> **"A DIFFERENT POPULAR MANTRA SAYS THAT IF YOU GIVE MORE, THEN GOD WILL MAKE YOU RICH."**

The hardest pressure inducement of them all is that if you love God, you will want to make God happy. If you don't, then God will feel bad but, you don't want God to feel bad, so you *will give more so that He won't feel bad anymore.*

But—your lack of financial giving is not the problem! Rather, it is just a *symptom* of the problem. (Mark 12:41-44, Luke 21:1-4)

You need to realize that:
- God is generous to you, (Eph 2:4-10) beyond all you can think or imagine. (1 Cor 2:7-13)

- He has been merciful to you, heaped grace upon you, (Eph 2:4-10) adopted you as His child, (Rom 8:15) and
- made you His steward. (1 Cor 4:1-2)

He did this:
- so you could invest the gifts and possessions that He has given you here on earth (Matt 25:14-30) for an eternal significance, (Rev 2:7, 10-11, 17, 26-29; 3:5, 12, 21)
- knowing that
    - by faith you allow the Holy Spirit to work through your life, (2 Cor 5:6-10)
    - you will receive rewards which will impact how you spend eternity! (Rev 2:7, 10-11, 17, 26-29; 3:5, 12)

Once you understand these truths, giving money (or anything else He has given you in trust as His steward for His purposes) will take care of itself, because you will be more and more attentive to how the Holy Spirit is directing your life and His resources. Once you begin allowing Him to direct the management of your time, talent, treasures, understanding, and relationships, then money (and the rest of this list of His possessions) becomes just a convenient tool to faithfully serve and transfer His assets into the lives of others in a way that will make an eternal difference. Go back and take a look at the eight generous lives I've shared with you. Where do you see yourself in them? Where could you start? What else would God have you direct into an active Kingdom purpose?

Several years ago, I helped organize a meeting of high-net-worth couples to discuss their lives and how they could use the assets God had given them, such as their time, talents, treasure, understanding, and relationships, to better serve the Lord's Kingdom. We went through a series of teachings and worship revealing the principles I've written about here.

One night, entirely without my knowledge or personal prodding, one couple stood together and made this statement. "My wife and I have been very blessed in our lives and business. We have no children, and our only family has more money than we do. So, we have decided to change our estate and start giving it all away to the Lord until it's gone. As we learned yesterday, it was HIS (the Lord's) all along." (Psa 50:10-15)

"MY WIFE AND I HAVE BEEN VERY BLESSED IN OUR LIVES AND BUSINESS. WE HAVE NO CHILDREN, AND OUR ONLY FAMILY HAS MORE MONEY THAN WE DO. SO, WE HAVE DECIDED TO CHANGE OUR ESTATE AND START GIVING IT ALL AWAY TO THE LORD UNTIL IT'S GONE. AS WE LEARNED, IT WAS HIS (THE LORD'S) ALL ALONG."

Overnight, this couple went from being, by all accounts "faithful givers," giving from their wealth, 10 to 20 percent of it – to giving everything they had and more to Kingdom purposes. It's close to what is referred to as "reverse tithing" – a tithe being ten percent of income – and it's definitely where you should start, but God has actually called you to let it all go. Change your lifestyle, live more modestly, surrender more and more to Him. It's all His anyway, so why not just be free and faithful with it all? (Jas 1:12; Rev 2:10)

My goal for you is that you will radically surrender it all. (Gal 2:20)

Perhaps you need to start with a tithe, but maybe a plan to move to 20, 50, or the 90%, "reverse tithe." The more you give what is His back to God, the more your life is filled with joy. (Phil 4:4)

The Rest of the Story...

Remember how I told you about my poor stewardship and the consequences of those poor decisions? I also shared some wonderful benefits that came from that hard season, eternal benefits that I will cherish for the rest of my life and into eternity. There was something I left out of my story, so far – something that God did just for me.

As you can imagine, there were a lot of stories and official reports written about me. But the hardest and the darkest point came when I read the Federal Government's recommendation that I receive 84 to 120 months in prison. I'll be the first to admit that the recommendation scared me. It was difficult reading the things written in that report: the mischaracterizations, the lies, about who I was. Most had come – unexamined and without any independent investigation or confirmation – from the many months of faulty media coverage. But now that they were all collected and included in this one report, I was afraid they would become my life story even though it wasn't actually the real story of my life.

I had spent my whole adult life helping people, living modestly, even generously. I had raised two wonderful young men. I had an outstanding marriage for over 34 years. I know God had used me powerfully to benefit many lives. With this one report, all of that seemed to be gone. I just sat on my couch and cried. I was inconsolable – for at that moment, I felt like my life had amounted to nothing, at least according to that official, Federal Government document.

But the Lord did for me something that I could not.

About a year later, after much legal wrangling, I stood before a Federal Judge to be sentenced. By this point, all the details had been worked out and, as mentioned before, that I would be facing just 30 months – two and a half years. I wasn't thrilled because even that wasn't fair. I was certainly happy not to be facing 120 months – ten years – in prison, but I did see it as the beginning of my miracle.

As we were ushered into the lobby of the courtroom, in its gallery there were friendly faces everywhere. Not just my family, but business people, pastors, homeless people, husbands and wives, recovering addicts, poor, rich, new friends and old. Some had flown in from across the country. Some had requested to call in from out of state to tell the judge about how my life had impacted theirs positively. Even one of the ex-wives of the Haiti project's CEO came. All of them hoped to stand before the judge and testify that this – "the who" that I was portrayed to be in the Federal Government's damning report – wasn't true, wasn't me, and wasn't Whose I truly am. The courtroom gallery was packed with people who supported me!

One by one, they stood before the judge and told their stories:
- A couple shared how my patient counseling had saved their marriage.
- A once-homeless man told a story of how I put him and his young daughter in a house we had 15-years ago so they could get out of the car they were living in.
- A single woman shared how I twice helped rescue her and her kids out of a terribly abusive relationship.
- Several pastors shared from first-hand experience the

impact of my life on the community.
- An ex-addict told the judge that I found him in a park and talked him into rehab. Then I drove him there, and he watched, astonished, as I reached into my own pocket and paid for it. It so touched him that he has never used drugs again and has been clean now for 16+ years. What was funny is that I didn't remember the incident at all.

There were so many people and stories that the judge put a stop to it for the sake of time. Did their stories matter to the Court, to the Federal prosecutor, to the media? It didn't seem so, but it did matter to me. And God knew it would: right there in front of me was hard evidence that my life did matter. And it was true. I had been living generously – imperfectly, but without reservation. I was thankful.

> **"I HAD BEEN LIVING GENEROUSLY - IMPERFECTLY, BUT WITHOUT RESERVATION. I WAS THANKFUL."**

Purpose and Passion

What do each of these eight stories – and countless others – have in common that causes the people in them to live consistently without reservation?

It begins with an understanding of their **purpose** – the motivation behind why they live without reservation. Their purpose is rooted in who they are and Whose they are. It's a deep, soulful understanding of who God has made them to be and what God did by generously, sacrificially, and lovingly giving His Son to pay for their sins. (John 3:16ff; 1 Cor 20-31) The generous life they now live is just the natural by-product of gratitude welling up from their deep understanding of God's generosity toward them.

Now, can someone live without reservation without understanding his or her purpose? Probably not. Sure, they can act generously, but they won't live without holding back. (Rom 12:1)

In my 20-plus years as a fundraiser, I have seen it all. And, not long into my career, I began to see people would readily give money and time for all kinds of reasons. Most decisions are emotional – driven by guilt or mercy. Sometimes, decisions come from a sense of duty. A good fundraiser will take full advantage of all of those emotions, specifically designing campaigns that push each emotional button to bring about a donation. The techniques are subtle, but the manipulation is powerful and present.

As an example, let me draw your attention to one of the most gut-wrenching campaign methods used today. Have you been able to avoid this one on your TV? The scene: A cold and starving dog shivers in his cage as the voiceover, usually a paid celebrity, describes the desperate, deplorable life this animal is facing. Then your senses become overwhelmed as one hopeless, innocent animal after another, flashes across the screen. Then comes the face of that voice-over you've been listening to, and you recognize her as someone you have seen before, someone trusted, as she explains how your monthly donation of "*just $19.00*" will save this dog and many other animals just like it. Consciously, you may not have noticed (but, your ear has) that the music has become lighter, more hopeful, as the spokesperson began to make her appeal for your action. The manipulation is there, in subtle, but clear ways that are almost impossible to detect unless you know what to look for. Nevertheless, it's there. Every second of that commercial has been designed to play to and pull on your emotions. The colors, images, music, paid endorser, website name, and even the monthly donation amount is tested and re-tested to get the highest financial response possible.

Ironically though, this particular commercial is also one of the most despised on television. Why? Because it's so intensely heartbreaking and so sad that it's hurtful to watch. But that is *also* part of the method used by the benefiting organization that sponsors the commercial! Does it work? Sure, it's marketing. It's a numbers game that will return a whopping two to five-percent over cost.

You read that right. By the time they pay the entire overhead, only about 95 cents per donation will go to presumably helping the animals. The other $18.05 got you to act. Do you see it? The purpose is to help the animals. Your emotions are played to motivate you, but it takes significant effort to get you to act upon this motivation. I am not critical of those who love and support animals. This technique is used thousands of different ways, by both Christian and secular organizations.

My hope is to deepen your understanding of why we live

generously. For the Christian to live generously, your purpose is established and rooted – not in some*thing* (our played emotions) – but rather, in what some*one* else, namely Jesus Christ, did for us.

Our passion is to steward our lives in the manner our Master desires. (Rom 12:1-2; 2 Cor 3:18)

In Psalm 33, King David's heart sings to his Creator – the one Who preserves him. David sings to Him a "new song" and "shouts with joy." I can just picture David – in my minds-eye – dancing, whirling around, singing, and shouting praises of joy in utter abandonment to the Lord God.

What brings such **passion** to you? Or, as Steve Jobs asked in his famous commencement speech to Stanford University graduates in 2005:

"What makes your heart SING?"

If you dig deep into that soulful purpose inside yourself, can you identify the unique and meaningful connection that just lights you up?

Now, here is where most Christians say something like, "living for Jesus does it" – but, that's the **purpose**. *How* does God, the Father, the Holy Spirit, and Jesus want you to live that purpose without reservation? This ***passion*** is the hallmark of your generous life, but keep in mind that what fires you up might not be so obvious.

Remember my eight examples of lives without reservation? Without knowing these eight folks, you would think that their passion was about feeding people, educating them, providing medical care for others, *etc.*, but it's not. If you talked to each of these visionaries, they would say their passion is about releasing the God-breathed potential that every believer has through Jesus Christ. It's just that each of them is doing it in their own way, each uniquely different.

In our modern society, we tend to equate thinking, success, and achievement by our *doing*, and not by our *releasing* and allowing God to do. (Phil 4:8)

> **"IN OUR MODERN SOCIETY, WE TEND TO EQUATE THINKING, SUCCESS, AND ACHIEVEMENT BY OUR DOING, AND NOT BY OUR RELEASING AND ALLOWING GOD TO DO."**

I mentioned operating a homeless mission years ago. While there, I often measured success by the numbers: how many we fed, housed, supplied basic needs to, or provided recovery programs for. I would report this data to my board, our donors, and to the public, as requested or required. It became my achievement measuring stick. But it was not my passion, and that was shown to me one day when I was at the local Home Depot's customer service counter.

The young woman helping me asked, "You're Mike Stickler, aren't you?"

"Yes," I replied, not sure where this was going.

"You saved my life. You took me in when I had nowhere to go. You gave me a home, food, clothing – for me and for my two kids. But most importantly, you gave me hope. I was at the lowest place in my life, my boyfriend had kicked me out on the street, and I was desperately trying to survive and help my children survive. You gave me a chance and I took it. I got my life together, by the grace of God, got clean and sober, and got back to living again. Now I am in training to be a manager here at Home Depot. Thank You!"

I didn't know what to say. After so many years, I didn't actually remember her. But that experience, and many more like it, fueled my passion. Her life made *MY* heart sing, and I could have danced like David! Her story was the "new song" in my heart.

My passion is for every person with whom I come into contact – to help them make their heart sing. No matter what my situation or location, whether I am in prison, or speaking to thousands in a convention center, I want to see a "new song" written upon their hearts.

I'll ask it again. What is your passion? If your passion does not inspire you, you will be ineffective in inspiring others with it. You'll just give the numbers, the statistics of what you are doing, in a perfunctory manner.

Your passion is neither a hobby nor your job. But your passion is intensely meaningful to your identity in Christ. Once you identify what makes your heart sing, then you will be able to allow that passion to inspire others. Your passion engages it. Empowers it. Drives it.

If you haven't found your passion yet, keep looking!

Chapter 7: Living a Life Without Reservation

Seek it!

Don't settle.

Don't get discouraged.

Don't stop – until you FIND IT!

As with all matters of the Master's design you'll know it when you are there!

Chapter 8
HAVING A VISION

I hope that by now you want to live a life like at least one of the generous lives I've previously described. My wife and I seek to pattern our lives after as these eight friends of mine, but that leads to one question …

Where do you start?

Well, you start with a vision. (Prov 29:18)

A vision is not a dream. A vision is not a set of goals. Instead, a vision is a "future destination" stated as *"where* you want to be and *when* you want to be there."

Think of it like taking a big, fun trip, let's say, to Hawaii.

> **"THINK OF IT LIKE TAKING A BIG, FUN TRIP, LET'S SAY, TO HAWAII."**

THE HAWAIIAN FAMILY VACATION

Now, if you could sit down with your family and ask them, **"Do you want to go on vacation?"** Just by throwing out the idea, even before asking the family to pray about their answer, you'll immediately hear all kinds of responses all beginning with YES!! And then the suggestions ranging from "Disneyland!" to "the North Pole!" from "camping!" to "a cruise!"

Now that process is called Dreaming Together. Incredibly fun, but it only produces a dream.

A "vision" is much more than a dream. It is a concrete description of the new "place where you want to be." A place that is well enough defined that it inspires you to *want* to go there and inspires you to *plan how* you will get there, your travel schedule, and *what* you will do once you arrive.

And vision-making is a bit more deliberate than Dreaming Together. It involves key decision makers (who, in your family, of course, could be everyone) in focused discussion to produce a tangible product. That product is the written vision for the family that will inspire, motivate and guide its actions toward this well-defined future "place."

Please note that "place," as used here, is really a metaphor for the content of most visions. It is used here to give a familiar reference term to the real concept of a vision's content: the new and better set of life-quality conditions for the community and its members, which are served by the organization (here, the family).

Now in our Hawaiian Vacation example, let's go back to the concept of the proposed vacation and ask the fundamental *"WHY?"* question.

The *"WHY?"* question: What is your **purpose** for taking a vacation? While the kids may have one or several reasons for their responses, you and your spouse may have the practical reasons pretty well in mind:

- Remove ourselves from our work-a-day place and its circumstances which have drained our energies and interest. (This is our **mission**, something we will *do*.)
- Immerse ourselves at our vacation spot in activities completely different from the activities we do each day at home. (This is also our **mission**, something else we will *do*.)
- Bring back to our lives at home: renewed spirits, broadened perspectives, re-charged energies, renewed interest, and some really positive attitudes. (This is our **purpose**.)
- Become re-focused, re-energized, and re-equipped for re-engaging our home's challenges, work, and life. (And this is our **vision**: *how we will be* when we're done.)

So, how do we make the vision statement inspiring to all of us?

Your first step is pulling the family together, asking: **"Where would you like us all to go?"**

Notice the subtle difference between *"Would* you like to go on vacation?" and *"Where would* you like to go on vacation?". **The initial question** is generic regarding the concept of "vacation," and got the family engaged in dreaming up possibilities! This **follow-up question** is more specific and focuses on the "destination."

This destination question requires the family to narrow the discussion by throwing out ideas that begin to play off each other. You'll hear some patterns develop, such as warm places, oceans, water, resorts, and beauty. In our example, as you consider all the suggestions and criteria, you come to realize that Hawaii fits all of them, so let's go there for our vacation! In other words, "Hawaii" seems to be the place that lets everyone get what they want in a manner most enjoyable to all. Plus, it adds some "pizzazz" to the practical purpose of this vacation, while promising a fun time for everyone!

Now, you've never been to Hawaii, so you need to conduct some research on which island or islands to visit, how to get there and back, the best time of year to travel, where to stay, reservations, costs, what the islands offer to vacationers and the time needed to see the sights. You will want to explore something new, learn about the islands, and pick the activities and relaxation of interest to your family. It's important to plan the time to get rested and refreshed, ready to return to life at home, too! The search begins, and the information rolls in.

So, after a bit, when enough information is gathered, you reconvene your group to discuss the research results and deal with the "how" of all this actually happening. You develop a timeline with benchmarks (or steps) and intermediate goals that will get you to Hawaii, entertain, challenge, and grow each of you while you are there, and get you all back home. Together, you:

- Develop a budget that will let you properly enjoy the trip.
- Decide how much time you need to experience your destination fully (one week? two?)
- Decide what you will have to prepare and bring to enjoy your time there.
- Recalculate the budget and timeline to agree with the time and travel constraints.
- Consider any hindrances, like conflicting commitments, *etc.*
- Again, recalculate the budget and timeline to agree with the intruding activity constraints.
- Set dates and the route of benchmarks to track your progress against the plan.
- Have one final meeting and memorialize your vision into a plan.

Once you all agree to make it public, have a kick-off party and invite your family and friends (in business, your entire organization – in your church, your entire congregation) into the vision. Invite everyone who will be going with you or will be happy that you are going, so they can catch the vision and support it, too. This is the beginning of the implementation stage.

Maybe you can update this entire group from time-to-time and update them on the progress that is being made as your plan rolls out. You made your budget, you bought the tickets, *etc.*, and you are celebrating and thanking God all along the way.

Periodically, re-cast your vision, re-stating in new words and excitement where you're going and why. Help everyone see it. You'll feel like you're repeating yourself—and you are, but that's okay. We all need to be reminded, to stay excited, to "catch the buzz!" So, it's important to hear testimonies of how great and beautiful Hawaii is and why Hawaii – and the things you can do there – are worth the trip.

> "YOU'LL FEEL LIKE YOU'RE REPEATING YOURSELF – AND YOU ARE, BUT THAT'S OK."

Always keep the vision before the group. Remember, hearing about Hawaii is not the same as being there for the first time, sinking your toes in the sand, walking in the warm water. Once you've been there, you'll be the one giving the testimonies!

And, there is one other thing: In every step of this process, include God and find His will for the change He wants for you and your family while on this vacation!

To illustrate the difference between Dreaming Together and Vision Making, the process I have just described here is a *decision* process. It is appropriate for making group decisions on issues where knowing God's will is not difficult because as the issue is clear and His will and commandments concerning how to handle it are also clear and not controversial. This happens less often than you think, but becomes second nature as the group and its members mature in their Christian walk.

"GODLY VISIONEERING"

Godly vision making – or "Godly visioneering" – to mimic Disney's term, "Imagineering" – determinedly seeks God's will for the tough decisions! Visioneering requires prayer, scripture, the correct circumstance, the counsel of mature Christians, the counsel of the

Church, and checking it against scripture *again*, even if you think your near-final draft has "got it." Although its steps are close to the decision process above, this process is for *discernment* (or discovering) of God's will by those charged with the governance of His organization. For example, a dedicated family, as in Joshua 24:15, a similarly dedicated business, or His Church (the Body of Christ) here on earth and local congregations of His Church – for discerning God's vision for His organization, whichever of these examples it may be.

By way of definition, "mature Christians" are those who have lived Godly lives for a long time and are consistent in their thinking and applying God's direction to their lives in His love.

"BY WAY OF DEFINITION, *"MATURE CHRISTIANS"* ARE THOSE WHO HAVE LIVED GODLY LIVES FOR A LONG TIME AND ARE CONSISTENT IN THEIR THINKING AND APPLYING GOD'S DIRECTION TO THEIR LIVES IN HIS LOVE."

This is the *discernment* process I want you and your family to use in developing the vision for your business, church, family, and for your personal life. Remember, you are His steward, (1 Cor 4:1-2; 1 Pet 4:10; Tit 1:7) so you'd better include Him early on and throughout each step, ever-seeking (and listening for) His will during this process.

Here is how I have helped many families, companies, and churches discern God's vision for their future, using the process outlined above:

1. Pull together your key decision makers and begin discussing what change all of you think God wants the organization to make. This can be in the organization, itself, in the community where it resides and serves, or wherever He wants to lead *His* organization to live out His purposes, and when He wants it to be done. In your business, these key decision makers might be the board or the senior management team. In your church, these could be the elders, the senior staff, or perhaps members of the congregation who have exercised the spiritual gift of discernment.

First, we prime the creative pump through discussion, teaching, or even reading this book. Then, the group takes a day together, in focused isolation at a house, hotel, the beach or somewhere no one will bother them.

When you get there, the leader collects everyone's cell phone and laptop both for safekeeping and to limit their distraction.

Then, as a group, you begin in prayer, then discussion, and more teaching, if needed.

About mid-day, break for individual time alone from the group. Have each person take their Bible and writing instruments. This is their personal time to ask the Lord where He wants to take each individual, family, and organization. Have all write down their ideas and His responses.

Yes, they all have to spend some time listening *for* and listening *to* His responses. Here's how:

- Once you feel that you have completed laying it out before Him in prayer, open your Bible and do some reading,
- Ask the Holy Spirit to confirm through the Word of God where He wants to take you,
- Write down what He seems to be telling you or guiding you to, and
- Check it against Scripture.

When you reconvene, begin with a prayer together to focus your effort and then openly share what you have written by yourselves during your "alone time" with God.

If you follow this procedure, you and your team will be astounded at the clear direction you have been given *together* by the Lord!

2. While still together, begin a brainstorming session on how to articulate what God has brought to you. Begin to kick around ideas as a group. The group's collective vision (this "new place" you are articulating) should aim to be the grandest accomplishment imaginable (if the need for change is there) or for how things are in the community your organization serves, so don't let obstacles such as money, talent, or anything else, inhibit this session. If thoughts come to mind that are an impediment like "I would love to achieve this or do that, but we don't have that kind of money," then ask yourself and the group one question: "After all, if God is in this, can't He or won't He fund it, supply the talent, or bring everyone together?" You get the idea. As you brainstorm, write your ideas on a dry erase board or large piece of paper. As you look

at them, you'll start to see trends and similarities. The more specific you are, the more easily this will come together.

3. Continue to use this decision-making process and enhance it by including focused conversations with God and checking their results against His word in Scripture. Do this to seek God's will at each step where there is uncertainty and insecurity within the group about the clarity of the issue or of God's will and His commandments regarding the issue. Tailor your *discernment* process for the issue and the spiritual maturity of the group.

Three Real-Life Examples

Here are some real-life examples of this process at work in which I have been involved:

A company decided to adopt a ten-square-block residential area just east of their campus. Their vision was to identify and meet every practical need of the families living in that area. The inhabitants of those ten square blocks were primarily relatively-recent Asian immigrants, and this became a big deal because the company employees were mostly white and Hispanics who commuted there from the suburbs. Ultimately, they developed a food ministry, classes in ESL (English as a Second Language), and attainment of U.S. citizenship. They used the appropriate business leaders they knew to mentor Asian entrepreneurs. They even set up a free medical clinic. They took every practical step the Lord led them to do to help the immigrants who lived in those ten square blocks. By involving their entire company in this neighborhood adoption, they taught, encouraged, and celebrated generosity in every segment of their business community. It wasn't just a project, but became a way of life for every member of the company as the corporate group culture grew into its vision. Now, this business is known for its generosity throughout the city. Not just for the money given, but for the innovative and purposeful services offered to make a significant difference in this community, benefiting everyone.

In Indiana, the Fischer family saw a need to which they intuitively knew God wanted them to respond. Brett Fischer is a physical therapist (PT) specializing in treating children with physical disabilities. Over the years as a PT, he began to see that not only were these children suffering because of their impairments, but their entire families were also in distress. Using the discernment process described above, the Fischer family began asking God how to help the "whole family" who has a disabled child or children. Where did it lead? Now, every year they take his patients' families camping. But their camping trips are very different from the usual "canoe and tent" experience. Each family has more than 50 volunteers helping them by making meals, providing marriage counseling, budget planning, respite care, and in-home physical therapy training. The volunteers, many of them professionals, provide for every need imaginable for each family. The best

> **"EACH FAMILY HAS MORE THAN 50 VOLUNTEERS HELPING THEM BY MAKING MEALS, PROVIDING MARRIAGE COUNSELING, BUDGET PLANNING, RESPITE CARE, AND IN-HOME THERAPY TRAINING."**

part is that those support relationships continue well after the camping trip ends. All thanks to the vision God gave Brett Fischer and his family.

With a gulp of conviction at their forgetfulness, the leadership of Cape Christian Church in South Florida realized that they hadn't asked God whether their building plans for the church's new home on their newly-purchased property were HIS plans. So, just weeks before they were to begin their expansion, they took it before the Lord in prayer and fasting. God made it clear He had a different idea in mind about what to do with the property they had just purchased to expand their campus upon: Give it away! Well, give some of it away, anyway. They went to the city manager and asked, "What does the city need?" After some thought, the city manager said, "We need parks. Parks where families can go to enjoy the south Florida weather together as a family." And so, under God's direction and with the city's expressed community need, Cape Christian turned five acres of their land into a park. A park for *everyone* to enjoy. This one act of generosity so-astounded the community, that the national media picked up on it. This park led to the "Not in Our Backyard" initiative, which set out to make sure that every school-age child in their city had what they needed to succeed and even go to college. The church provided books, tutors, a medical clinic, back-to-school clothes and literally everything any child would need to be successful. As a by-product of this church's generosity, attendance grew by 60% in one year, which caused them to return to the Lord (first, this time) for HIS guidance on how to faithfully accommodate and serve the new members ... but, that's another story.

CASTING YOUR VISION

"Vision only lasts 30 days." ~ George Barna

Remember, your vision needs to always stay firmly before you, your family, and your team. If it does not, you tend to get "vision drift," that loss of focus even to the point of losing sight of where you wanted to go and when you wanted to get there.

You need to cast, broadcast, and re-broadcast your vision every 30 days, according to contemporary Christian attitude pollster, George Barna's astute observation. Why? Because otherwise, you will begin to get off course. When sailing, a good sailor checks his navigation every hour. Why? Because if he doesn't, he may find himself so far off course, it will take hours to get back on track. If he stays off long enough, he'll miss his destination all together!

Casting your vision isn't really all that hard, and it doesn't need to be all that formal, either. But it has to be done. You can do it at the dinner table, or in staff and board meetings, even just by reporting on your progress or asking what others have done. You can do it by including it in your newsletter, in your blog, on your webpage or simply including it in prayer time (an oft-forgotten forum). You'll feel like you're repeating yourself – because you are. And you are because you need to be. It's okay. Your vision needs to be reinforced over and over and over again.

Remind everyone what it's about why you all got together and decided upon this vision.

Celebrate the progress and individual acts of generosity. Use every opportunity to rejoice by announcing how many meals you've served, by calling out the volunteers and thanking them, or simply reporting how much money was given to the cause. Celebration is crucial. Few things are as motivating as a celebrated vision, shared often.

It is astounding how God will use personal testimonies to not only motivate you, but draw others into the vision as well. If possible, have your employees, volunteers, family members, and team members share their testimonies about how participating in this quest for your vision is affecting their lives. Be sure to use video and written testimonies, as well as live testimonies, and share them on your social media accounts.

You also need to commit a budget to your vision. Without leadership and budget, you are not taking your vision seriously, and it will fail in time. In your family the leader is usually one of the parents. In a business or church, assign this stewardship task to a senior staff member. This vision-champion must have the authority and resources to drive the vision forward, organize its prime movers and doers; create its celebrations and testimonies. The vision should be treated with the respect of any other department or aspect of corporate, church, or family life. Above all, remember that discerned correctly, God's purpose for you and your organization is to achieve His vision.

Start Small, Learn as you Grow, Grow as you Learn

Does this feel a little overwhelming? Honestly, it should. If it's underwhelming, or without risk, it doesn't take faith. On the other hand, I have seen great value in small starts. Let's think that through.

Two "Small Start" Examples

I remember back in the '90s when I was running the homeless mission, a man called and said, "I want to bring my kids down and serve a meal." He reasoned that his children could see how people in poverty live. Our program manager told him "no thank you." Taken aback, he asked, "Why? Don't you need volunteers?" "Yes, we do," she replied, "but, if you want to help, why not have your family make a meal and bring it down? Then sit and dine with us, our family and yours?" Her

> **"... BUT IF YOU WANT TO HELP, WHY NOT HAVE YOUR FAMILY MAKE A MEAL AND BRING IT DOWN? THEN SIT AND DINE WITH US, OUR FAMILY AND YOURS."**

reasoning: this much-fuller involvement would be more effective toward both his goals and for the mission's goals as well. He loved the idea more than his own of merely meeting a goal. He loved it for the experience! Just that one idea – that change in perspective – turned what would have been a "spectator sport" into a real sacrifice-to-service experience. It involved their meal planning and preparation (including the labor and needed materials), and person-to-person involvement for serving it and then talking to the shelter residents, person-to-person. It would involve

Chapter 8: Having a Vision

the time, treasure, talent, understanding, and relationships God gave them for service to others. It made all the difference in the world. So, think through how to start, but always keep your vision before you as you go.

In Dallas, Texas, a woman[1] I know wanted to wash the feet of the homeless. She wasn't quite sure how to start, but one Christmas she just gathered up some warm socks, hats, and mittens, and found some homeless people. She asked first, "Could you use some warm socks, a hat, some mittens?" When they responded "yes," she would kneel down, unlace their shoes, and pull off their dirty shoes and socks. Then out came the wash basin, warm water, and clean towels. After she was through cleaning up and drying their feet, she would slip on the nice, new, warm socks. Often, she would look up only to see them sobbing quietly at her kindness. From these small beginnings of a life without reservation, others came forth, and a contagious desire for more soon developed. On hearing of her service, her friends wanted to join in, then church groups and local businesses. Today, during the Christmas season, hundreds of volunteers wash the feet of thousands of homeless people in Texas.

> **"DURING THE CHRISTMAS SEASON, HUNDREDS OF VOLUNTEERS WASH THE FEET OF THOUSANDS OF HOMELESS PEOPLE IN TEXAS."**

WHAT TO DO FIRST

It occurs to me that some of you would like to just write a check. Maybe you are one who feels you are a steward of your excess cash or of windfall revenue only. Don't you do it! Not yet, anyway. Just writing a check will cut your blessing short. Likewise, it will cut short the blessing to the recipient.

Once you have your vision, your leadership, budget, and a small beginning, then you need to practice some due diligence. Ultimately, you need to become an expert in the area you want to serve. Begin by researching the subject and what has been done and what is currently effective. Talk to community leaders, asking them what's needed. Interview and tour the top facilities or programs in the area that are doing similar work. In addition, take video, pictures, and good notes. Find out what your church is doing or wants to do. Do they have a

---

1 Susie Jennings; https://operationcareinternational.org

similar vision? Don't leave one stone unturned in your endeavor to secure a clear picture of what is really happening through similar efforts. This task can take months to complete, but it is necessary.

> Suppose one of you wants to build a tower. Won't you first sit down and estimate the cost to see if you have enough money to complete it? For if you lay the foundation and are not able to finish it, everyone who sees it will ridicule you, saying, "This person began to build and wasn't able to finish."
> – Luke 14:28-30 (NIV)

By practicing due diligence, your vision will solidify. Prayerfully consider how your approach may be different and unique. Let me explain: I don't know any Bible-believing church body that doesn't say they have a vision for discipleship. Yet study after study demonstrates that most churches do not have a formal discipleship process. They will direct those in need to Bible studies, pulpit teachings, home group meeting and even Bible Schools. All are good.

But, let me share another vision for making disciples. Imagine you are 15-25 years old. You're in the prime of your life, about to enter into the world making a living, getting married, and having a family. You've been brought up in the church and love Jesus. But nearly every study says most young adults at this age lose their way through college,[2] the opposite sex, and worldly attractions. These distractions lure their hearts and minds away from all they've learned in the church groups of their youth. In time, most lose their way and somehow leave their love for Jesus behind.

But imagine that there's an opportunity placed before some of these young adults: the chance to set sail on a tall sailing ship for three or four months. While aboard, they are personally discipled in the Word of God, taught the ways of the Lord and experience the Holy Spirit leading and directing their lives every day. All the while at sea, they are learning the work ethic of running the ship and what it means to be responsible for the lives of others aboard as they travel from island to island. Not only do they man the ships helm, when ashore they share the gospel with the locals and do service projects, including providing

---

2 <u>Soul Searching: The Religious and Spiritual Lives of American Teenagers</u> Christian Smith and Melinda Lundquist Denton, Oxford University Press, 2005

necessities to the island peoples. When they return home, they have had an encounter with the Living God.

Now that's discipleship that will last!

> **"WHEN THEY RETURN HOME, THEY HAVE HAD AN ENCOUNTER WITH THE LIVING GOD."**

See the difference? Someone reading this might say; "Mike, not everyone can do that." Why not? It just takes some organization and a few dollars. "Mike, not everyone likes boats, let alone can sail!" Okay, there are hundreds of effective groups doing innovative and proven work in this area. Do your due diligence. Once you have, join in with one of them, or if there is none, start something new.

Whatever you do, find where God is working and join with Him. After all, if you're going to put God's time, talents, treasure, understanding, and relationships into this project, then shouldn't it be extraordinary? Shouldn't it be demonstrating the generous God we serve?

Make a Generosity Plan

Now that you have a solid purpose of living a life without reservation, you need a plan to get to your "new place" destination. Remember my story about going to Hawaii? If you're taking a trip you need to do a few things:

1. Define the "new place:" ***Vision***. With God's leading, decide what changes need to be made in the circumstances of the community and its members whom you will serve, and in what part of this change you will act to make it happen.
2. How you're going to get there: ***Mission***. Address what you, along with the help of others, are going do in order to make the change you and God agree needs to be made.
3. Articulate what's important to you and God about how you do these things: ***Values***. *How* you do *what* you do is important – you may be the only Bible others ever read.
4. Compass, map, and timepiece for the trip: ***Goals and their measurement***. Know the track to success in your and God's plans, keep on track, and celebrate accomplishments along the way!

MISSION AND VISION

There is much written and taught about the concepts of "mission" and "vision." It's my opinion that much of it confuses "mission" with "vision" and *vice versa*. They are clearly distinct and different elements of your generosity plan.

As stated, your **vision** is where the Lord wants you to "go," *and* what the Lord wants you to change. The **mission** is what you do, the vehicle to get you "there," *to* make and continue making changes.

Think about it like this: if you're going to Hawaii for a vacation in order to return home refreshed and ready to face life at home anew, there are several ways to travel there.

- You could fly commercially, as millions do.
- You could decide to take a cruise, a motor yacht, or a sailboat.
- You could even try to paddle a canoe, as some have attempted to do.

The way you get there also depends upon several factors such as cost, ability, knowledge, skills, and even your health. Sailing to Hawaii will require very different physical abilities than flying there commercially.

Another factor related to your mission is time. How much time you have could dictate your method, as can time measured in age. For example, if you are of retirement age, you have less remaining of your lifespan than if you are of college age. Also, as a general rule, the less time you have, the more money a vision takes.

I also want you to remember that your mission (method) can change, but generally, your vision won't – until it is accomplished. You might start out with one mission – washing feet for example – and over time your part in that mission might change to recruiting hundreds of volunteers to wash feet. The vision to bring service – and by so doing, show God's love to the homeless in your community – remains the same.

VALUES

These are what is important and acceptable to God as you represent Him by what you do.

There are many ways to love the homeless. For my friend, it is showing Jesus' example by washing the feet of society's "dirty people." By washing feet, you can demonstrate God's love, humility, and generosity. The recipient receives being valued, being cleaned, and the practical comfort of warm socks. It's a value that she doesn't want to be forgotten. All of her volunteers are trained in washing feet, and once trained, expected to humble themselves in this fashion.

Others value equality, empathy, education, unity, and a growing understanding in the Word of God. The Calvary Chapel Movement values verse-by-verse teaching in the Holy Scriptures. Prison Fellowship values completing its work through members of the local church. The Fisher family values healing for the patient's entire family along with healing children with disabilities.

What is the non-negotiable value that you want to be the hallmark of your life without reservation?

> **"WHAT IS THE NON-NEGOTIABLE VALUE THAT YOU WANT TO BE THE HALLMARK OF YOUR LIFE WITHOUT RESERVATION?"**

GOALS

The goals of your life-plan need to be viewed as the benchmarks, or the orderly completion of certain activities along the way to getting to the "destination," or making any changes God wants to be made. They are used to keep the activity accomplished and on track to achieve the vision. Remember, it's like the ship's navigator who records its position consistently while sailing the course in order to make the necessary adjustments to remain on track.

Keep track of how closely you meet your goals. When you meet the goals, that is how you know you're making progress with God's vision for your life.

- A goal may be based on financial plans. For example: We want to be able to give 50% of our income to Kingdom purposes in 10 years and 90% in 15 years.
- A goal may be based on the numbers served. Example: We want to wash the feet of 500 homeless per year by 2025, 1000 homeless by 2030, 2000 homeless by 2035.

- A goal may be based on actions. Example: A church wants to invite 1000 families to visit them by Christmas this year, and 2000 by next ... and 5000 by Christmas, five years from now.

See how goals will begin to help you set and keep your course? Your goals can have sub-layers, which are useful for managing activity too. Example: We want to wash the feet of 500 homeless per year by 2025, which will take 100 volunteers. This example makes you face two objectives, recruiting 100 volunteers and locating 500 homeless to serve. A sub-layered goal will then drive the logistics of how to accomplish it through your mission.

Remember, your goals need to be God-sized and just outside what seems possible for you, but not for God.

In summary, your goals must have these criteria:

- Lead to the overall vision.
- Define the mission.
- Serve within your values.
- Be written.
- Be shared with all stakeholders.
- Its achievement must be celebrated.

Chapter 9
CELEBRATING GENEROSITY

Why is it important to celebrate generosity? Doesn't the Bible teach that we should keep our giving quiet and not let the left hand know what the right hand is doing? (Matt 6:1-4)

The Bible does teach that. It also teaches us to give honor where honor is due. (Rom 13:7)

So, which is it?

Both.

HUMILITY CHECK

Nearly three decades ago, I was attending a men's Bible study at a local hospital. It was similar to the hundreds of men's morning studies I have attended around the country. We would gather, order breakfast, facilitate the subject, read the verses of the day, then eventually share our thoughts.

One day, one of the elder members, a solid man of God, took a few minutes to congratulate me on the progress and understanding I had gained in the short time he had known me.

My response: "It's the Lord. He is just using me, just praise Him."

Shortly after that, the meeting closed, we all paid our checks, and left.

That particular day, I had come to the meeting with my mentor, Art Barkley. Art, by then, was a retired missionary with New Tribes Mission, my spiritual father, who spent years discipling me. His was a faithful voice in my life, then and even today, as he has poured his life into mine.

As we rode home together, he began one of many discussions I will never forget: "Mike, do you remember the positive comments that were said about you today?"

"Sure," I said.

"Do you remember what you said in response?"

"I think so, why?"

Art went on; "You rambled on about how it was all the Lord, and we should give Him all the glory or something like that."

"What's wrong with that?" I interjected, surprised and slightly offended by his tone and where this seemed to be going.

"The problem is that it was false humility! Everyone in that room knows it is God working in you. You don't need to state the obvious. By doing so, you're just trying to look humble and deflect the genuine thankfulness these men were trying to convey. It was ugly."

> **"THE PROBLEM IS THAT IT WAS FALSE HUMILITY! EVERYONE IN THAT ROOM KNOWS IT IS GOD WORKING IN YOU. YOU DON'T NEED TO STATE THE OBVIOUS."**

I sat there in silence feeling very convicted. After what seemed like hours, I mustered the courage to ask him one clarifying question "What should I have said?"

"Mike, the Bible says give honor to whom honor is due. Just a simple "thank you" is always best."

I let that sink in. Now, and over the years since that ride home, my only response to gratitude expressed towards me is a simple and sincere, "Thank You!" along with a smile. What the Holy Spirit did that day, so many years ago, was expose my heart. My heart was full of pride, in this case, spiritual pride, but pride none-the-less. Think about it. I was masking that spiritual pride by acting "spiritual" – in a proud and false way, as Art pointed out! Sometimes I forget how wicked my heart can be. (Jer 17:9-10)

In the first four verses of Matthew Chapter 6, Jesus speaks of a prideful heart in terms of our motives when He tells us to not "sound a trumpet, as the hypocrites do" ... to get attention to our charitable actions, but go about it quietly without the expectation of gratitude, recognition, or celebration.

Does that mean the receiver or those who see the act of generosity shouldn't be grateful, recognizing what the Lord has done through the giver's obedience? Shouldn't *we* celebrate with a pure heart?

Of course, we should. As always, it's the heart's condition in the action that counts, celebrating generosity is simply giving honor where honor is due. (Rom 13:7) Properly done, it becomes a powerful testimony that encourages the generosity of others. (Matt 5:16)

Celebrate Generosity

It is crucial to incorporate the celebration of kindness into your generosity plan. So, how do you do that?

Remember that key phrase from my friend Norm Miller, "Keep your eyes open and your ear to the ground." You need to watch and listen for generous actions that are by faith. A gift given, courage demonstrated, a quiet act of service, forgiveness in the hardest of times, obedience to the Holy Spirit, ... When you see or hear of generosity, make a way to celebrate it!

One morning, I was at my favorite bagel shop when a homeless guy came in. He went right over to the coffee bar and poured himself a cup of coffee. The coffee there wasn't free, but he had his own cup, so he helped himself, and sat down. He just wanted to get warm, be inside, and wake up. Sleeping on the streets is difficult. It's cold. The ground is as hard as concrete and filthy dirty, not to mention it is unsafe. Let's just say it's not conducive to a good night's sleep! So often, part of the ritual of the homeless is to warm-up in the morning.

It was busy in the restaurant that day, and I was one of the few who noticed him. I waded through the crowd over to his table, bent over, and asked, "Are you hungry?"

"No, no," he replied, not sure of my motives.

"I'm going to get something for myself, may I get you something?" I pressed on.

"Well ... ok ... anything, anything would be fine," he replied, still very hesitant.

"How about a bacon and egg bagel sandwich?" I continued, "Those are good, I have them all the time."

Finally, he mumbled, "Sure," still seeming to be bothered by the whole encounter.

I returned with a bacon and egg bagel, orange juice, and a cup for the coffee. That way the coffee he'd already taken was paid for.

"Thanks," he grumbled without even looking up.

I returned to my table and friends. They were engrossed in their conversation and didn't even seem to notice my absence. A few minutes later, I glanced over to see if my new homeless friend was still at his table, but he was gone. The table was clear, and the food, plate, and cups were gone. I returned my attention to my friends and the discussion. Twenty minutes later, we finished our breakfast and concluded our conversation. We hugged, said our goodbyes, and started for the exit.

Out of the corner of my eye, I caught a glimpse of a figure approaching, a handsome, well-dressed woman, obviously a business professional of some sort.

"Hey ... hey, mister," she called, with a tone that suggested urgency.

Had I dropped my wallet or something? I turned to face her, raising my eyebrows with a quizzical "what do you want" look.

As she got closer, she said, "I saw what you did."

"I'm sorry?" I queried, without really knowing what this was all about.

"I saw what you did with that homeless man. Thank you."

"Sure," I replied, relieved that this encounter was not going as badly as I was afraid it might.

Then she added, "Nobody seems to care about those people (I hate that term "those people"), it's nice to see you do, thank you."

Now she had put a big smile on her face as she extended her hand to shake mine. As I reached for her hand with both of mine, I said, "You're welcome," as warmly as I knew how. Then I turned, awkwardly, and headed out the door, across the parking lot, and to my car.

As I sat quietly in the car, I thought, 'What was that all about? Kind of weird.' Then, the thought came right behind it: 'Your love and generosity were not only for the homeless man, they were for her to see.' At that moment, I realized the power of celebrating generosity. It's not only for you and the one toward whom you were generous. God has used you to be generous *and* to demonstrate generosity. And, all three of you have been blessed through your act. Celebrating generosity can even be *primarily* for "building up" a third party: those watching.

> **"YOUR LOVE AND GENEROSITY WERE NOT ONLY FOR THE HOMELESS MAN, THEY WERE FOR HER TO SEE."**

When we celebrate generosity, we motivate others with the

grace of God. (Rom 6:17–18) Celebrating generosity realigns their thinking to where it belongs: that we all have a greater purpose in life. It *gives permission* to be generous—and that's contagious. The hesitance shattered by your generosity, makes them now realize that not only do they *want* to be generous, they will now realize that it's *okay* to be generous, too. Powerful stuff!

Keep in mind, though, that seeing generous living 'out loud' dissipates quickly, it needs to be connected to a purpose – as soon as possible – to last. It's always best to present an opportunity to be generous with a plan of action. It could be a need for a volunteer or financial giving, or for merely joining a generosity movement once its observing party self-identifies and comments on your act. Wherever God is leading you, just remember, celebrating generosity is crucial to you, your family, your church, your business, and your community.

Celebration Ideas

There is an old horse-training adage: Make the wrong thing difficult and the right thing easy.

Now, before you start sending me letters and emails about how people are not horses, here is the idea I want you to digest:

Because of the fall of man, (Gen 3:1-7) all human beings long to fulfill their need for acceptance, significance, and security, but, only a restored relationship with our Creator can satisfy this. That restoration can only come from the payment for our sin made by Jesus on the cross. (Rom 5:12-19) We just need to be reminded of that fact – *often*, *constantly* and *endlessly*.

We all need to be encouraged to do the "right thing" of living generously – constantly bearing in mind that the "right thing" is always opposed, overtly and subtly, by an endless drumbeat of selfishness (*i.e.*, doing the *wrong things*), as encouraged by the world, the flesh and the devil. (1 John 2:15-17)

Face-to-face

Constant, simple *acknowledgment* celebrations: "thank you," or "well done," are the baseline.

A step up might be: drawing others' attention to generous acts, saying "thank you" in front of others, and making connective introductions like: "have you all met John here? One of his deep passions is for feeding poor families," or "Jerry and Susie have just returned from San Salvador, and they have been sharing with me what God is doing down there. It's amazing! I encourage you to take them out to lunch and receive the blessing, too."

How about putting a 15-year-old young believer on the stage of your church, and allow him to give a testimony of his summer in Russia, where he and other youth shared the gospel on the streets of Moscow? I remember one church had their entire youth group stand up in front of the congregation, each holding a picture of the children they sponsored. At the same time, the pastor elaborated on this act of faith, sacrifice, and lifetime commitment that each of these youths personally made to sponsor a child. Before that Sunday concluded, more than a hundred families committed to sponsoring nearly 150 more children. These are wonderful examples of grace, purpose and the contagiousness that generosity brings.

But what about more ways to celebrate with even greater reach?

Social media

With social media, you have powerful tools at your fingertips, 24/7, to share your celebration stories. The camera in your phone allows you to capture those celebration stories in picture or video and share them with the world on Facebook, Twitter, Instagram, or other social media. Longer videos can be posted on your web page or YouTube.

Write a blog to celebrate your generosity story with passion! Our website, GenerousLife.net, is always looking for good stories to post. Our radio program loves showcasing great generosity interviews.

If you practice celebrating generosity, you will discover more opportunities than you can ever imagine. Keep in mind that you're telling stories, so share personal and inspiring, narratives.

Parties and recognition

The best celebrations honor the person on their terms.
For example:

A touching story was shown on TV a while ago, about a beloved high school janitor whom the school wanted to honor and thank.[1] To do it, the kids formed a committee, who recruited volunteers to decorate the gym. Their parents made goodies for the party, all of which was to celebrate the generosity of this one, unassuming man. Yet, they took

---
1 CBS Sunday Morning; https://www.youtube.com/watch?v=FPVGznxirn4

it a step further. They found out that the janitor had always wanted to go skydiving, so the kids raised the few hundred dollars it took to send him skydiving. As you can expect, this was caught on video by the yearbook team and shared via social media. And yes, they cleaned up the gym after the party concluded, as yet another well-treasured present for their janitor! Celebrating generosity by being generous. You've got to love it! I know God does.

In Los Angeles, I have a friend who raises support for a large children's charity. One year, a woman donated a particularly-needed, one-time gift of $250,000. My friend wanted to find a way to celebrate this amazing and timely gift. Knowing this generous woman was a big fan of a particular fashion designer in Beverly Hills, she contacted the designer's offices, relayed the story of her gift and how it would be used, and made a humble proposition.

Impressed with the story of this donation and how it would help the charity serve the children, the designer gladly agreed to thank her for them. He had the donor picked up in a limousine and brought to their studios, where my friend and the donor were seated in an over-stuffed couch. The designer then gave her a preview of the spring clothing line he was about to unveil.

Imagine my friend, this generous donor and favorite designer, sipping wine as one model after another came out from the backstage showing off the never-seen-before season's collection!

Then, as the donor focused in on one or two outfits she just loved, the designer leaned over and said; "I want to thank you personally for what you have done for the children, these two ensembles are for you."

"No, no, I couldn't!" resisted the donor.

"I insist," replied the designer.

Before the day was over, the donor was fitted for her two outfits, and within a week, they were delivered to her home. She was ecstatic! And now, every time she wears one of those two outfits, she remembers the story of how loved and appreciated she feels as a result of the designer's generous response to the story of her gift.

This one act of celebrating her generosity did not cost my friend or her charity one cent. The designer donated the whole thing. Why? Because he was so impressed with this one woman's story of significant generosity, it inspired *him!* He was also well aware it couldn't hurt having a woman with that kind of influence and affluence raving about him and his designs to all of her friends. And the charity won a life-long donor.

Note that these celebrations generated more grace, more purpose, more passion, more *generosity*, and became more inspirational as more and more people became involved.

My last thought concerning celebrating generosity is this: All the telling of stories, the thanking people, the affirmation of others that we've talked about in this chapter are, as such celebrations need to be, an extension of the gratitude for what God has done for you through His Son, Jesus Christ. (John 3:16)

- You should forgive much because you have been forgiven much. (Matt 6:14)
- You should love much because you have been loved much. (Matt 5:43-45)
- You should generously give much because you have been generously given much. (Luke 6:37-38; 2 Cor 9:6ff)

Now that is something to ***celebrate***!

What to do Tomorrow

In the preceding chapters,
- I have given you an outline that you need to fill in with the details of your own life.
- I have given you the Biblical principles and mandates with many examples of generous lives that I've experienced first-hand.
- I have poured out my heart and soul to you through this book because I passionately believe this world needs more generosity.

Just watch the news for twenty minutes, Google current events, or even look at the Christian-media commentary on those events, and you'll see a clear and decisive *lack* of generosity shown to one another. Honestly, I have a hard time seeing the life of Christ lived out in the lives of most Christians today. I write this not to indict the church, but rather to press every reader into action, into change, into living differently – into living without reservation!

Chapter 9: Celebrating Generosity

With these last few words, I appeal to you: please, when you finish your first-read of this book, do not just put it down and say to yourself, "Hmm, that was good" (assuming you liked this book). I am praying you'll do something tomorrow with all that you have learned.

But, what?

Well, I have a vision:
> I can see every household in America
> step out in faith
> with one ordinary act of generosity
> in their community.

Just one act – that is what I am praying for.

Start small, but, *start ... tomorrow*. Now, you and I can each do at least <u>one</u> ordinary act of generosity in a day – right? So, you and me, lets each do one tomorrow! And also, starting tomorrow, *smile* – as much as you can. You have much to be smiling about! Much to be joyful for.

But, today – Day One – I want you to plan at least your family's first vision meeting, as we discussed in Chapter 8. Take the time to get your family (at least), your business, and church team on board with why this meeting will be important for them.

And: Oh! Continue doing your ordinary act of generosity with me each day this week. Why? Studies in human behavior show that to effect a change by turning an action into a lifestyle, you need to do it every day for forty or more days. So, keep going!

So, tomorrow, Day Two. Each of us could:
- Have coffee with that person you've been avoiding. Just sit and actively listen to them. Keep doing it until your heart begins to change about them.
- Buy a stranger a cup of coffee for no reason other than you want to. You could even suggest that they 'pay it forward' with someone they don't know, too.
- Give the panhandler you see so often a buck or two. And when you see them the next day, ask if they're hungry, then sit with them and eat together.
- Stop and visit that guy at the office with whom you are

annoyed. Just visit with him.
- Call your pastor's office and make an appointment. When you meet, talk about this book and what you've been reading and how you want to be of service there. Then, by faith, just go and do it. Leave a copy of this book with them. Believe me, they'll be curious as to what motivated such a meeting. Trust me, most of their appointments do not take such a turn. Most appointments with pastors are a cry for help, rather than an offer *to* help.

Day Three: Go to your local Christian bookstore or our website (GenerousLife.net) and order a copy of *A Journey to Generosity* which will guide you through more generosity ideas for the next 41 days and beyond.

Day Four: After you finish your first-read of this book, review the five areas of life over which our Master has charged us with stewardship of the assets He has entrusted to us: time, talent, treasure, understanding, and relationships. Prayerfully consider how He wants you to manage those areas with the expectancy of His imminent return. Keep a journal of what you discover.

1. Time:

Time is the governor of all we do. It is the only item of the five we get from God that we will not get more of, so it is and should be the most precious commodity. Ask the Holy Spirit to reveal to you how you are wasting the time He has given you, how you have dedicated and used this time poorly, and how the time you have been given should be invested in-and-for Kingdom purposes. Learn from this (it's like the *listening* part of prayer) about where you can use your time for much better purposes.

Caution: We often will go to amazing lengths to justify our misuse of time. We say things like; "The poker game I go to is part of my efforts to evangelize," or, "Lunch with my old college girlfriends is the way I show them I haven't changed since becoming a Christian." Just be honest before God and allow *Him* to determine the best use of HIS time. Listen for His response. Write down what He shows you. Check it against Scripture. Now, do what He says!

2. Talent

Talent is what God has given and uniquely built into you – and what amazing gifts these special abilities are! The question is: are you using them for His purposes as He designed? I know professional athletes who use their amazing athletic gifts to connect with disadvantaged youth at sports camps. They have found a way to use what God has given them to bless people and give all the glory to God. You can do that too. Take your talents: professional, artistic, physical, and mental – along with your spiritual gifts – and give them back to God. You can serve your church and community by participating in a ministry, wherever God leads.

Just remember these easy rules:
- Find where God is already at work and join Him in it.
- Serve where you are celebrated, not where you will only be tolerated.
- Don't hold back. Serve 100% as unto the Lord.

3. Treasure

Treasure is frequently written about. Most pastors avoid talking about "money" because it is the god of our age. And, people – Christians – don't like to be told by someone else how to use "their" money. As with the other four assets on this list, the money you have is not yours either. It's God's, and you have been entrusted with it as a steward, to use ONLY as *He* directs. Honestly, you can't mess this up if you honorably keep this attitude of faithfulness.

Some Christian leaders teach that the tithe is 'old covenant,' while others teach that "gifts of grace" are all you need to give.

Here is what I want you to do. Go to your pastor and ask him what he teaches regarding giving. Then be like a Berean (read about them in Acts, Chapter 17) and study the Bible (Acts 17:10-12) to show yourself approved. (2 Tim 2:15) Money is a hard issue only because we get so tangled up in it. Get yourself untangled by knowing the truth, and the truth will set you free. (John 8:32) Again, as I said earlier, if you have HIS attitude that it all belongs to HIM, (Psa 50:7-15) then you can't really mess this up.

At this time in our lives, Kim and I shoot for the financial goal of being 'reverse tithers.' Our goal is to free up 90% of our income in order to steward as much for our Master's purpose as possible, then, with us to live off the remaining 10%. We have listed the priorities for our stewardship as follows:

1. 10% of our gross income goes to our local church.
2. Pay off all debt using the "snowball method" as taught by Dave Ramsey (see DaveRamsey.com).
3. Maintain earthly savings, investments and insurance to cover the foreseen and unforeseen expenses of our lives, after which we can (or must) turn from working to produce income. Upon death, the residual goes to Kingdom purposes.
4. Set yearly goals of spending less, giving more, and – as our debt gets paid off and investments reach maturity – dedicate the greater liquidity and equity to provide additional funds for investing in Kingdom purposes.
5. Every dollar goes to our generosity vision. Giving as God directs, this increases yearly, with our prime goal remaining at 90% of all our income to be used and given to Kingdom purposes.

Okay, someone out there is saying, "this is a crazy plan," or "there are better ways to plan your life financially."

I have two responses.
- First, it's <u>not my life</u>: it's His. He'll adjust it as He sees fit.
- And, second, if I remember it's all His, I can't mess it up, even if it seems crazy.

Remember: This is an issue of faith, ***not*** about worldly economics. God doesn't need your or my money. He desires for you and me to trust Him, and to let Him bless us and others through us, by submitting ourselves to His plan and His leading in our lives.

4. Understanding

Understanding is that which God gives you through His Holy Spirit. (John 14:26; Eph 1:7-9; 2 Tim 2:7) The understanding of Who He is, Whose you are, His creation, and His purpose for you – in other words, the big questions of life!

This, in my view, is the most neglected stewardship area of our lives regarding accountability. I think there is a BIG misunderstanding in modern society that says "the more we learn, the more we are given" – where in truth, it is: "the more we share our understanding and give it away to others, the more we are given to share with others." (John 16:13-15)

Think about it like this: Today, we Christians have more access to inspirational and powerful Biblical teaching, writing, and training than ever before in human history (except, maybe those three years walking with Jesus, when He was here on earth). Today, with the click of a button, we have access to all of God's word in a very long list of exceptional translations, early church teachings, systematic theology and volumes of commentaries, not to mention the websites and live-streaming of modern preachers and teachers of the Word of God. Yet time and time again, study upon study shows that contemporary Christians cannot answer the most fundamental questions of what Christ has done for us through the cross of Calvary. (Eph 1:1-11)

It seems to me, that if <u>access</u> to the information was all we needed, then we should be the most spiritually mature and healthy Christians in all history! But look around you ... we're not. (James 1:22)

Even more evident is the lack of faith in so many Christians' walk. (1 Tim 4:1-15; Heb 3:12-19) Why is this? Because we don't trust Him. We don't believe His Word. We seldom, if ever, "get in the wheelbarrow and ride!" It leads us all into living a barren experience, merely existing rather than living the generous "life without reservation" that God intended: The Promised Land.

It's a two-part equation:

UNDERSTANDING =
KNOWING GOD THROUGH STUDY OF HIS WORD
+
TRUSTING THAT KNOWLEDGE WITH ACTION

Those two parts of the equation are what we need to share – without reservation! As we learn through good Bible teaching, reading great Christian books, the study of His Word, and through the loving discipling of mature Christians, our hearts and minds begin to be filled with who God is, and Whose He has made us to be. Moreover, we need to take that knowledge and put it to work by trusting Him, thus using that knowledge.

For example: The Holy Spirit may remind us that we need to resolve an unresolved issue with a coworker. (1 Thes 5:12; Eph 4:31-32) Maybe, it's a minor thing, and that co-worker has not said anything to you about it. You reason, "It's no big deal – probably forgotten." But the situation is nagging at you. So, by faith, you wander into his office cubical, apologize, and clear the air. It turns out to be a powerful moment for both of you as your co-worker explains just how much this meant to him. Now, you walk away with the joy of the Lord in your heart. (Gal 5:16-24)

So, What Now?

First, I want to commend you for getting into the wheelbarrow and riding! It was risky. That's why it took faith. And it was worth it because you experienced God first-hand (2 Cor 3:16-18) and gained understanding. It's that understanding you now need to generously share with others. (2 Cor 9:6ff) Personally, I think that this is why the Church today is not as spiritually mature as it could be. We consume, and consume, and consume all this great knowledge, but we don't share any of what we've taken in by putting that knowledge into action by faith. (James 2:14-26) But, when we do – as in the simple illustration above – we gain understanding.

So, what should we do with that understanding?

Give it away![2] Tell others what you now realize. Teach it to your children. (Eph 1:7-19; Col 1:9-12; Col 2:2-3) I don't know how you will do it, but do it your way, (Tit 2:11-15; Acts 11:23) and do it generously. (Rom 12:4-8) When you do, others will be blessed, their faith will grow, (Heb 10:24-25; 1 Pet 2:5) and they, too, will get in the wheelbarrow. Oh ... and God will reward you with *more* understanding. (Luke 19:17-19; 1 John 5:20)

Be faithful with little and much will be given to you. (Matt 25:21-23)

5. Relationships

Back in 1999, a local pastor said to me, "Mike, the only things that are eternal are relationships—first, our relationship with God and then our relationship with one another."

Clearly, as I have said in the preceding pages, there are certainly other eternal things in life, but I see his point. If we do not first allow the Holy Spirit to manage His relationship with us, (Eph 4:30; Psa 78:40; Heb 3:16-19) then we will not experience the generous life that God has

---

[2] https://www.youtube.com/watch?v=mUfcasIspAY. Gaither Vocal Band, Ernie Haase & Signature Sound - Give It Away [Live]

desired and designed specifically for each of us. (Rom 8:30)

But we have an additional stewardship responsibility with the earthly relationships (Rom 14:12) we develop throughout our lives. You could argue that the Apostle Paul ended each of his epistles instructing the churches in relationship management. And more importantly, Jesus' "red-letter" instructions (in some Bibles, *all of Jesus' words* are all printed in red) either addressed our relating with God the Father or relating with one another. It's fair to say that the totality of Scripture is devoted to practical, relational living that is eternal in its impact, accountability, and scope. (2 Tim 3:16)

It is why our eternal rewards will be measured by the relationships where we follow the leading of the Holy Spirit (1Cor 4:1-4; Matt 5:12; Luke 6:35) in our daily lives rather than following the leading of our own design. Those rewards will somehow have something powerfully to do with our heavenly relationship to God, (Rev 3:5-6, 10-12, 21-22; Rev 22:12) and impact us for all of eternity. (Rev 22:14-17) This is something I readily admit that I do not fully understand.

Yet it becomes clear to even the most cursory observer that, as Christians, we need to pay attention and focus on our relationships more effectively and fervently, because today the Christian community seems to reflect a casual worldly pattern in how we treat one another.

This is especially true in the areas of marriage, family, conflict, forgiveness and reconciliation. These are often neglected, not

> **"SOME ACTUALLY SPEND THEIR ENTIRE CHRISTIAN LIFE DESTROYING EVERY HUMAN BEING WITH WHICH THEY COME IN CONTACT, LEAVING A WAKE OF DEEPLY-HURT PEOPLE BEHIND THEM."**

just by individuals, but by entire congregations and denominations, too. The divorce rate continues to climb as men and women disregard their promises (2 Tim 3:1-7) to one another and seek their selfish desire. (2 Tim 3:1-7) Some actually spend their entire Christian life destroying every human being with which they come into contact, leaving a wake of deeply-hurt people behind them. No relationship seems to be immune from the hurt, whether they be with spouses, siblings, children, personal friends, business, church, or other acquaintances. Ultimately no one is spared the wide swath of devastation. Yet God's generous grace is freely offered to each of us. (2 Pet 3:9) His love covers a multitude of sins. (1 Pet 4:8)

Relationship Priority – With God

First and foremost, we have a relationship with the Lord, our God (Col 1:9-12) to nurture and grow. This is a wonderful mystery (Col 1:26-27) and is always a pursuit—never an arrival. It involves the same elements of relationship-building that are necessary to any meaningful relationship in our lives, except that our partner in this relationship, the Holy Spirit, is always available to us and is anxious to love and build into that relationship.

There are volumes upon volumes of commentaries written about knowing God. But, sometimes, I believe, we over-think it. And, often we end up with an artificial, formulaic list of things we need to do to deepen our relationship with HIM. Things like prayer, Bible reading, going to church and Christian service all too often become a list of things that "good Christians" (John 15:5) do that are woven into our week. Rote – not faithful – for seldom is our heart in it.

Just imagine if you told your spouse that you would show them your love by sitting down and talking with them – precisely at 6:00 am for a half hour every morning. First, you would read parts of their past letters to you (randomly or systematically), and then, have the conversation. It would be deep and meaningful and comprised primarily of a list of needs and/or complaints, with a couple "thanks" in there for good measure. Of course, you will do all talking and close it off before your spouse can even respond, let alone have a chance to process, what you've said. Think how that would build and maintain a warm and loving relationship with your spouse. I'm afraid that it would quickly and certainly affect your relationship's growth – and not in a good way. Your hearts and your relationship would grow, all right: colder.

Naturally, we understand that the most meaningful, intimate, and nurturing conversations we have usually arise from a sort of intentional spontaneity, just finding time in the moment of life together to share hearts, challenges, encouragement, affection, day's activities, and so on. That is what I believe Paul was thinking when he told the church in Thessalonica to pray *without ceasing*. Please don't misinterpret this to think that I'm saying prayer is bad. I'm not. What I am saying is often prayer becomes rote, rigid and cold. I want to set you free from rote,

> **"... OFTEN PRAYER BECOMES ROTE, RIGID AND COLD."**

rigid and cold – and enable you to enjoy a growing relationship with the God of the universe.

Let me explain it like this: One day my wife, Kim, and I had just an incredible day together. We had been married a number of years, so the "newness" of our marriage relationship had passed, but not our passion for one another. By all outside appearances, we'd had just an average day, shopping, chores, lunch together, holding hands, being together, sharing hearts, and connecting with one another. When we returned home, we were putting groceries away and the joy of our relationship just continued even through this mundane chore.

As we remained playful and affectionate through these chores, at one point we were just playfully wrestling around in the kitchen and I grabbed her up in my arms, she looked up at me and said; "Mike, you sure know how to get me."

"Get me? What do you mean?" I honestly responded.

"You know …" she said, "You know how to touch my heart."

Later, with growing curiosity, I asked her what I did, specifically, that stirred such a close connection. (I wanted to know exactly the formula I stumbled across in order to put in my arsenal for later use.) She laughed, "Mike, you can't duplicate what happened today with a set of planned steps. That would be artificial. It wasn't one thing you did; it was all of it. It was you and me just being together. It was your focus on 'us' – that is how you get me."

I am embarrassed to say that at the time I didn't understand what she was saying, but over the years since, it's begun to seep through my thick skull. It's about our heart connecting with our spouse's heart, growing and maturing *togetherness* in our relationship.

And, these same principles apply to our relationship with the Lord.

We should be committed to prayer not only because it's a duty (Luke 18:13-14) – a command to do – but, so we can grow closer to God, understand His heart, and find His will. It's a practice of unceasing connection. With formality sometimes, but more often, it is the deliberate spontaneity of listening and speaking and listening again, that allows us to touch hearts with Him. About now, someone is thinking, "Mike, which is it, planned or spontaneous?"

My answer is: "Yes! It's both. Just open your heart to His, share your love, fears, day, plans, decisions confusion, laughter and sorrows. But then *listen* to what He says in response. Remember, He died so you could have this relationship of intimacy. Use it! Enjoy it!"

Your Bible study habits align within these same principles. Reading and studying the Bible is also a duty and a command, (Luke 18:13-14) because it is essential to knowing and understanding this generous God of ours. God knows there is no other way. You should study His Living Word to draw closer to and understand how to better relate to Him. (James 4:8) Bible study is not an effort to master the subject within. You study the Bible to allow HIM to master *you*, to "put on the mind of Christ." (Rom 12:1-2) As described in Chapter 3, allow the Holy Spirit to change (renew) your mind, will and emotions, conforming (Rom 12:2) them to the image of Jesus Christ. (2 Cor 3:18)

Neither is study about "pleasing" God, as with some religious act of contrition. Rather, it is an act of love. I personally approach my Bible study the same way as my life-long study of my wife. It is a fabulous treasure hunt of uncovering the beauty of this person I love so much. (The Song of Solomon – *all* of it!)

Christian service is also often viewed as a duty, something we do in obedience to God's command. I truly despise such an idea, because acting to please God or obey Him is contrary to the Holy Spirit's intent. The Lord wants our service to be a by-product that pours from us out of our love for Him because He first loved us. (1 John) We minister, serve, and bear one another's burdens, (Gal 6:2) not because we are required to do so, but rather, because we *want* to do so.

> **"WE MINISTER, SERVE, AND BEAR ONE ANOTHER'S BURDENS, NOT BECAUSE WE ARE REQUIRED TO DO SO, BUT RATHER, BECAUSE WE *WANT* TO DO SO."**

"But Mike," you say, "we are commanded to be obedient!" (Rom 6:16) I agree, but obedience means agreeing with God both in our heart *and* by our actions. We desire to obey. Not to perform a trick or to respond to a command, like a dog. In that latter context, who would want to obey God?

When I was a younger man and newly married, my wife would ask me to do the dishes. I didn't like to do the dishes (yeah, I know, who does?). So, I would stall, ignore, wait her out, or whatever else I could think of in order not to do them. My heart wasn't trying to go against her. I just didn't want to be bothered by something I didn't like to do. That poor girl would try everything: bribery, anger, raising her voice, even begging. It became a contest of wills that was beginning to damage our relationship.

Then one day, we had some friends over for dinner. Kim planned a special dinner, complete with her special cheese puffs. This particular evening, she was rushing around, trying to pull it all together; but, was frustrated by her time constraints. Kim was just running out of time to complete everything before our guests were to arrive. Sensing her frustration, I suggested she forego the cheese puffs, reasoning that we have known this couple for many years, so they would understand. Her reply to my suggestion was "Mike, don't you know that this is the way I show them that I love them?"

With that, it clicked. I should serve Kim by doing the dishes because I love her and want to demonstrate that love to her in a tangible way. To this day, I still dislike doing the dishes (don't tell Kim – this is just between us, ok?). But I eagerly do them because of the deep affection I have for her.

Our relationship with God is something we can't take for granted, be slothful about, or worse, assume that it is totally dependent on Him to work out. It is a two-way street, and we have a responsibility to be wise stewards, even faithful investors in it. (Matt 25:25) It should come first in our lives above all other relationships.

Relationship Priority – Husbands and Wives

Our spouses should be a close second to God, our Creator, in our relationship priority. Here is a secret about marriage I learned from the ministry of Dennis and Barbara Rainey (FamilyLifeMinistries.org). Your spouse was a specific gift from God, (Eph 5) made and designed uniquely for you. (Gen 2:22) They have strengths to compliment your every weakness. (Gen 2:23) He knew perfectly what would complete you for life on earth. (Gen 2:15-25) If this statement is true (and it is), then you can trust Him, the Perfect Giver, to give you the perfect gift for your needs.

Now, close your eyes and picture in your mind your spouse's face. Ask yourself, can you trust the giver, rather than the gift? The marriage relationship in the modern world is one that, all too often, is fraught with fraud. We somehow believe our spouse is in our lives to make our life better, happier, and more pleasing for us. And, when that doesn't happen, and our perceived desires aren't met, then it's somehow ok to move on to someone else who will please us and meet those desires. Beyond that, in our hearts, we let the marriage relationship revolve around ourselves, rather than realizing that it is a stewardship responsibility.

> **"ASK YOURSELF, CAN YOU TRUST THE GIVER, RATHER THAN THE GIFT?"**

WAKE UP! This marriage relationship we have is God's. He gives it to us to manage and enjoy. Marriage is the model of how the Lord relates to His church. (Eph 5) Marriage, as He intends it, teaches us how to relate to God, what He truly expects from us, and how to steward (protect) our first priority, which is our relationship with God. Remember, in the garden, Eve was made to be Adam's *helper* – who could have known that this ancient marriage model was the "help" for which our modern "Eve" would be given to us modern "Adams?" In Ephesians 5, verses 22 and 23, Paul gives us a wonderful outline of how husbands and wives should relate to one another and to the Holy Spirit. Paul describes how wives should submit to their husbands and how husbands should lay down their lives for their wives. (Eph 5:25-28)

Right about now a woman or two out there is saying, "Whoa, no way am I going to submit to anyone!" Or, a husband is reading this saying, "Well, I'd give her more of my life if she'd _____ (*fill in the blank*)." But don't you both see, this is a mutual principle of God's design. It's part of trusting Him.

If you, husband, would unreservedly cherish your wife, surrounding her with love and safety, giving her your everything, (Eph 5:25; Col 3:18) then, she can't help but come under submission to your love (Song of Solomon – the whole book *again*!) and the laying down of your life for her as Christ died for the Church. (Eph 5:25) Why? Because you'll be trusting the Lord by giving her your everything. (Eph 5:31-32) She'll be trusting Christ through your example and will want to be in submission in everything.

So, my friend, this is the model, built on God's spiritual principle of "submission" upon which marriage is founded. It's always about trusting God, the giver, and not the gift.

> **"IT'S ALWAYS ABOUT TRUSTING GOD, THE GIVER, AND NOT THE GIFT."**

But wait! There's more! Look at Ephesians 5, verse 32:
> This is a profound mystery – I am talking about Christ and the church.

In this one simple verse – so easily overlooked – Paul reveals that this model is not just a model of the husband-wife relationship, but also THE model of how God relates to His church. This is, at once, both an ingenious and a practical revelation. If we want to know how to steward our relationship with God, we can look at our healthy, Biblically-submitted and everything-laid-down marriage. If I want to understand how to relate Biblically to my spouse, I need look no further than to Christ's example of His complete and utter self-sacrifice for His Church in going to the cross – in order to unlock the profound mystery of marriage stewardship. For that is the definition of true husband-wife love.

Relationship Priority – With Children from the beginning of humanity's walk on earth

Third in priority, is our relationship with our children. Unlike our marriage relationship, which is our only " … 'til death do us part" earthly relationship, our relationship with our children is designed to allow them, *themselves*, to grow apart from us – and ultimately, leave us – to "cleave" to another in marriage! (Gen 2:24) (Oh, that's right … just as we did with *our* parents – way back when we were growing up.)

Our children start out as infants who are solely dependent upon us, their parents. Then, with each day passing, they are on a journey of separation into adulthood with more and more independence from us, their parents, while developing more and more dependence upon God. A parent cannot hold onto them, nor should they try. (Gen 2:24) Our stewardship responsibility is to mold our children into healthy, generous stewards themselves. Keeping God's goal of mature adults in mind, we need to be used by the Holy Spirit in guiding them (Rom 8:14) through each stage of their life towards their adulthood.

Yet their independence shouldn't stop there. As they become adults, our role as parents changes from nurturing and teaching, to simply "being here," sharing in their life, guiding and mentoring them by example and in word, when asked, and assisting them to complete their stewardship responsibilities. (Eph 6:4) For this, *we* need the wisdom, patience, and the gentle guidance of the Holy Spirit. (Rom 8:26,27) As it was for our parents and will be for their's, in every stage of growth with our children, and even with all of the loving instruction we can get, parenting is "on-the-job-training."

Your children are His, to whom you have been given a direct stewardship responsibility for a time. Depend on Him to guide you, and He will be responsible for the results.

Like every parent, so every child is unique and different, as is every family and culture. However, the Lord is the same, yesterday, today, and forever. (Heb 13:8)

Be mindful of your stewardship of these three relationship priorities. Don't get them mixed up. You are always to remain a faithful steward of all of these relationships – for they are the Master's:

- The Lord always comes first.
- Your spouse is second.
- Following these would be your children and eventually their children.

Relationship Priority – With Others

In our stewardship of earthly relationships, we must use tremendous discernment and learn to completely trust the Holy Spirit's guidance as He instructs us in accordance to His Word. (John 16:13-15; 2 Tim 3:16) In the Second Epistle to the Church at Corinth, Paul instructs that we Christians are all given the ministry of reconciliation. (2 Cor 5:18)

- The first half of that ministry is that we are to be reconciled unto God; (Col 1:15-20; Rom 5:8-11; 2 Cor 5:20) which is His work of forgiveness. (2 Cor 5:19; Rom 3:23-26)
- The second half of that ministry is that we are to be reconciled unto one another. (Matt 5:24)

But what does that mean? Does it mean that I must like

everyone? Trust everyone? Let everyone into my close relationships? Before we appropriate a phrase here, like the Apostle Paul used many times "May it never be!" – we must recall Jesus' teaching as to who is our neighbor. (Luke 2:25-37) But what 'being reconciled to one unto another' does mean is, as with God, you must have no unresolved issues between you and your 'neighbor.' (Matt 5:24)

Here is how you'll know if any such issues exist.

Imagine you are at the grocery store, pushing your shopping cart through the aisles, enjoying a quick bit of shopping. As you round the end of one aisle into the next, you look up to see _____ (*insert their name here*). What is your first reaction? Can you push forward and greet them without any hesitancy? Or, is your immediate response to duck that aisle, or even to leave the store? But, wait. Think about it. What could happen? At most you'll greet them and exchange a few pleasantries. That is a very simple interaction with minimal risk of being hurt again.

Paul writes in Romans, "As far as it's concerned with you, be at peace with everyone." (Rom 12:18) In my view, if you can't move forward, go up the aisle, and have a reasonable, safe conversation, then you're not reconciled. You also need to see with your heart that this was not some accidental, chance encounter with them. You go nowhere by accident! There are no coincidences with God. (Psa 37:23) Our sovereign God orchestrates these circumstances to reveal our hearts, the other party's heart or *both* hearts. (Luke 6:45; Mark 7:20-23l; Eph 2:10) Maybe you are at "peace;" but, they are not, and God is using you for *their* benefit, or maybe God wants to reveal to both of you that all is at peace. It doesn't matter because this sovereign encounter is about trusting *God*, and not yourself or the other party. Our heavenly Father wants His children to be at peace with one another. (Rom 12:16) What good Father wouldn't?

If you are the one who wants to duck the aisle, what do you do to be reconciled to them?

First, be honest with yourself and the other person. Kindly say something like, "Mike, it's been a long time and seeing you here, like this, makes me realize that maybe we should talk some things through." See how they respond. If it is cautiously positive, then determine right there what are the next steps, such as meeting and talking another time. If the door is clearly closed on their part, then leave it open on your part, saying something like, "If you change your mind and want to reach out to me, that's okay just let me know." Remember, as far as it concerns you, (Rom 12:18) there's no scriptural admonition to force peace between parties.

What if you do duck the aisle? Or, even leave the store? It's okay. You just failed the test God put before you and, rest assured, you will be given the test again. At least you know there are areas of stewardship God wants you to work on. But it is now time to be prayerfully honest before the Lord. Pour out your hurts before him and ask Him what you should do next. Listen for and listen to His answer. Write it down. Check it against Scripture. Do what He wants you to do.

Understand that conflicts will happen. Jesus is aware of this. He humbled Himself to become the likeness of flesh, (Phil 2:5-8) so we would have an advocate with the Father. (1 John 2:1) You don't need to pretend to be holy. You are holy because He is Holy. (Lev 11:45) He is just using this conflict to mold you into His image. (Rom 8:29; 2 Cor 3:18) Let Him have His perfect way with you and do His perfect work in you. (James 1:2-4)

Maybe you need to forgive, pay restitution, (Matt 6:12-15; Exo 22:12) give mercy, or find grace in this situation. (Psa 103:8-14) It's your unbelief that is in the way of reconciliation.

Pray my favorite prayer: "Lord, help me with my unbelief" (Mark 9:24) and He will. What you do next, is … just get in the wheelbarrow.

Keeping Peace Before Making Peace is Required

Relationships are sometimes sticky, and the process of reconciliation is about making peace. It's hard, *full-on*, faith-work, at times. It's much easier to ignore the process and just keep the 'peace' you have. But as I said, conflict happens, and you shouldn't avoid it, rather, expect and embrace it when it comes. When you start to discern a lack of real peace in the relationship, acknowledge it early. If you, or someone you are in a relationship with, begin to feel unresolved issues, open an honest dialogue about it immediately. (Matt 5:25) Every time I've done this, I have been grateful. The conflict may have been difficult, but the resulting strengthening of the relationship was well worth it. If it is a more serious conflict in, perhaps, a formalized relationship, like a marriage vow or business contract, then find a way for more formal (but, Biblical) conflict resolution.

For more than 20 years, every contract drawn up by my Christian companies has included a "dispute clause" mandating a Christian arbitration between parties if a dispute were to arise. This panel consists of several arbitrators, including one pastor and one Christian businessman for each party in the dispute. They meet, hear all sides, resolve the conflict and any surrounding issues in accordance with the contract and Biblical principles, and then inform the parties of their decision. The contract makes this arbitration binding, meaning it is enforceable by a court of law. It removes all the name-calling, false-spiritualizing, and furthering the conflict through a long, drawn-out adversarial legal process. Plus, it is finalized by an arbitration decision document that is legal and binding.

Trust me, in every conflict you have something to learn. I especially like the idea that the panel can move quickly to a decision that may preserve the relationships between the parties. This mending is something that extended time in legal disputes works against. This arbitration process is all in the spirit of 1 Corinthians, Chapter 6; where the Apostle Paul admonishes church members not to sue one another. (1 Cor 6)

In my view, Paul doesn't forbid legal action, here, as one may occasionally need the help of the courts to enforce matters of dispute or other issues. Rather – and most importantly – resolving conflicts is to be done in a way that is God-honoring, endeavoring to preserve the relationship, (James 1:22-25; 2 Cor 9:6-15) while demonstrating proper stewardship. (Matt 5:37)

Money and Relationships

Take a close look at Matthew, Chapter 18, verses 21 through 35. (Go on, read it, I'll wait.) Often, the best and quickest way to resolve conflicts and preserve relationships is to forgive the central or related financial debt. In this passage, Jesus tells us about a servant who was forgiven a huge debt he could never have repaid. But that servant then turned around and would not forgive another who owed him a small amount and was not able to pay! Although this parable is clearly about forgiveness, it's also about gratitude, following the grace-model of generosity, and about preserving relationships. Jesus is simply using money, the god of His (and our) time on earth, to demonstrate these principles.

> **"GOD WOULD PREFER THAT YOU FORGIVE A FINANCIAL DEBT IN ORDER TO PRESERVE THE RELATIONSHIP BECAUSE IT'S *HIS* MONEY ANYWAY."**

I think that taking this passage in its literal sense is appropriate: when it comes to money, God would prefer that you forgive a financial debt in order to preserve the relationship because it's His money anyway. It was the Lord Who was cheated, swindled, or taken advantage of – not you. He will mete out His justice as He sees fit, something you and I are unable to do. So, it doesn't matter how much money is involved – let it go.

But, consider that this is also a parable – and that money is just a metaphor illustrating the cause of many conflicts. Applying Jesus' principles of forgiveness, gratitude, and repeating the grace-model of generosity in these conflicts are important as well.

I once had a client who owed me $100,000. It was clear that he couldn't repay it. I could have exercised the arbitration clause in his contract, sent him to collections, or even hired an attorney. Instead, I simply sent him a release that forgave the debt. When he received it, he called me in tears, thanking me for being so generous. I really couldn't say I'd done anything special. I just lived out the clear instruction from the Word of God, and, as a result, not only did we avoid conflicts with each other, we are still friends to this day.

On the other side of the coin (please pardon the pun), sometimes we become debtors, ourselves. And, if the one we owe refuses to forgive the debt, what then, is our responsibility?

Preserve the relationship.

Pay when and as much as you can until full restitution is made. Keep honest communications open. Make no promises you are not confident you can keep (Rom 12:1-2) and trust the Lord. No matter how much debtors pressure you, just rest in your Lord Jesus. Keep in mind, that the conflict you are experiencing may be because God is using you to conform the debtor into the image of Christ. (Rom 14:12; 1 Cor 4:1) It's always best not to get into debt at all, but at times we can all get into financial difficulties. When you do, the manner in which you handle yourself is also a stewardship issue (2 Cor 3:18; Rom 8.29) and can become a real testimony of generosity toward others, even though you are the one who owes.

Putting it All Together

Living a life without reservation and practicing generosity functions best as a whole entirety. Of course, it is only natural to be a better steward in a couple of areas while needing work on some others. Jesus alone was able to fully demonstrate a generous life in time, talent, treasure, understanding, and relationships – all at the same time – and in a holistic way. But that doesn't take away from our responsibility to allow the Holy Spirit to work in every area of our lives to be conforming us to Him. (1 Cor 4:1-2; 1 Pet 4:10) Remember, there's a war going on for our minds!

We should be mindful each day of the responsibility and privilege God has given us as His stewards: (Eph 1:3-6) We are to be faithful in the management of our daily lives to His glory, (Col 3:17; 1 Cor 4:1-2) as we are led by faith, (Gal 5:16ff) knowing that what we allow the Holy Spirit to do through our lives by faith will result in eternal rewards. (Rev 2:10, 11, 17, 26-29; 3:5, 6, 10-12, 21) And more importantly, they matter to our Heavenly Father, right now. (Rev 3:22, 22:12ff)

Chapter 10
ONE LAST STORY

Oskar was born and raised in Austria to strongly Catholic, deeply religious parents. His nearest neighbors were a Jewish family, including a rabbi with two sons, who became Oskar's best friends growing up. This upbringing set the stage for his life, one that would save more than 1,200 Jews from being sent to their deaths at the hands of the Nazis in World War concentration camps.

By all accounts, Oskar had many shortcomings. He grew up to be a braggart, bully, and womanizer. He loved to drink alcohol, but his favorite "drink" was to drink of the power and prestige of the times, which was fueled by the Nazis' rise to dominance in fall of 1939. At that time, Oskar Schindler moved to Krakow, purchased an enamelware company and started doing business with the Nazis.

Initially, Schindler's enamelware company employed only 150 Jewish slave laborers. But, by 1940, Krakow Jews were forced into an overcrowded ghetto and he could no longer overlook the systematic brutality and genocide of an entire race happening before his very eyes. Schindler began to use his contacts and well-known bravado to negotiate with the Austrian Waffen-SS Captain Amon Leopold Göth, the commandant of the nearby Plaszow labor camp.

Commandant Göth ruled the camp with an iron fist, publicly murdering – in one night – more than four thousand Jews who tried to hide from incarceration in the labor camp. Schindler ended up hiding about eleven hundred Jews from the camp by relocating them to his factory, where they received much better treatment than did the Plaszow labor camp's remaining population.

By 1944, the Germans were losing the war, and the Russians were closing in on Poland. Schindler persuaded Göth to allow him to move his factory and his workers to a safer site in Brunnlitz, Czechoslovakia, where they would manufacture military shell casings. Schindler convinced Göth to "sell" the workers to him, thus creating the famous Schindler's list that ultimately saved the lives of about 800 men and 300 women. The men safely arrived in Brunnlitz, but the women were mistakenly loaded on the train to Auschwitz,[16] where the Nazis murdered as many as four million people in the camp's gas chambers and ovens. Weeks later, using his bravado and plenty of cash bribes, Schindler had "his women" released to his charge, marking the *only* time that a train of living passengers ever left a death camp.

Abraham Zuberman, a Schindler Jew himself, recalled how Oskar Schindler got the 300 'Schindler women' released: "What people don't understand about Oskar is the power of the man, his strength, his determination. Everything he did to save the Jews. Can you imagine the power it took for him to pull out 300 people from Auschwitz? At Auschwitz there is only one way you got out, as we use to say, through a chimney! Understand?"

The Schindler women were being herded off toward the showers. They did not know whether it would be water or gas. "Then we heard a voice: 'What are you doing with these people? These are my people,'" reported Anna Duklauer Perl, one of the 300 women Auschwitz survivors. She never forgot his raspy voice when he, while surrounded by S.S. Guards, gave them his guarantee: "Now you are finally with me, you are safe now. Don't be afraid of anything. You don't have to worry anymore.

Poldek Pfefferberg, another Schindler Jew, recalled how, in 1944, Schindler was a very wealthy man, a multi-millionaire: "He could have taken the money and gone to Switzerland ... he could have bought Beverly Hills. But instead, he gambled his life and all of his money to save us." When Pfefferberg asked him, "Why?" Schindler answered, "There was no choice. If you saw a dog going to be crushed under a car, wouldn't you help him?"

Twenty years after the war, Moshe Bejski, another on Schindler's list and later a Supreme Court Justice in Israel, asked Oskar Schindler why he did it. Schindler replied, "I knew the people who worked for me. When you know people, you have to behave towards them like human beings." Oskar Schindler spent something like four million German Marks – an enormous sum at that time and the equivalent to about $260-millon-dollars today,

> **"I KNEW THE PEOPLE WHO WORKED FOR ME. WHEN YOU KNOW THE PEOPLE, YOU HAVE TO BEHAVE TOWARD THEM LIKE HUMAN BEINGS."**
>
> ~ OSKAR SCHINDLER

to keep Jews out of the death camps. He spent four years risking his life and nearly all his fortune to rescue them, and he did it openly.

He did it for strangers.[1]

In 1993, Steven Spielberg told the story of Oskar Schindler in his hugely successful film, *Schindler's List*.[2] It is one of my favorite movies: powerful, compelling, sobering. The final scene of the story is set in the evening hours in the courtyard of the Brunnlitz camp. Schindler and his wife, Emilie, exit his quarters, each carrying a small suitcase. In the dark, not too far from his Mercedes, stand twelve hundred workers. As the couple crosses the courtyard to the car, Itzhak Stern (a Jew who worked for Schindler) and Rabbi Menashe Levartov approach.

Levartov was a rabbi working for Amon Göth whom Schindler saved on multiple occasions. Göth personally attempted to kill him with two different pistols, but multiple shots jammed and Schindler had him brought to the enamel works as an "engineer," which of course Schindler knew he wasn't. They became good friends. Even after the factory closed in 1944 and Rabbi Levartov was headed to another concentration camp, Schindler intervened once again and saved his life.

The rabbi hands him some papers, saying, "We've written a letter trying to explain things," "In case you're captured. Every worker has signed it."

Oskar Schindler looks at the list of signatures that continues for several pages and then slips it in his pocket. "Thank you" replies Schindler. Then Stern steps forward and places a simple gold band, a ring into Schindler's hand. It looks like a wedding ring. Inside there is an inscription. It reads in Hebrew: "Whoever saves one life, saves the world." Schindler slips the ring on and admires it for a moment, then quietly thanks them both. He seems to withdraw and says to himself, "I could've got more out" … as he steps away from Stern, his wife, the car and the workers, … repeating, "I could've got more … if I'd just … I don't know, if I'd just … I could've got more." Stern isn't sure if he heard him right. "Oskar, there are twelve hundred people who are alive because of you. Look at them." He can't. "If I'd made more money … I threw away so much money, you have no idea. If I'd just …" says Schindler quietly.

"There will be generations because of what you did," presses Stern.

---

[1] United States Holocaust Memorial Museum: https://encyclopedia.ushmm.org/dcontent/en/article/oskar-schindler
[2] International Movie Database: https://www.imdb.com/title/tt0108052/

"I didn't do enough," mutters Schindler even more remorseful. "You did so much," Stern almost pleading.

Schindler begins to weep, Stern too. Schindler's face is apologetic as his eyes sweep across the faces of the workers, seemingly begging for forgiveness for not doing more.

Then Schindler, pointing at his car, says, "This car. Göth would've bought this car. Why did I keep it? Ten people right there. Ten more I could've got. This Pin," he adds, as he rips the elaborate swastika from his lapel, and holds it out to Stern apologetically. "Two people. This is gold. Two more people. He would've given me at least two for it. At least one... He would've given me one. One more. One more person. A person, Stern, for this. One more. I could've gotten one more person ... I didn't."

> **"I DIDN'T DO ENOUGH."**
>
> ~ OSKAR SCHINDLER

Now Schindler is weeping convulsively, all the emotion of all the years of guilt that has been consuming him. "They killed so many people ... they killed so many people."

The two weeping men embrace.

My friends, like Schindler, we too will weep. We will wish, no matter how many lives we impacted, that we had done more, and every life, everything, will not be enough as we stand before Jesus.

Chapter 10: One Last Story

Now go.
Live a *Life Without Reservation* with passion and generosity!

TAKE A 41-DAY JOURNEY...

...a journey that will deepen your life and impact your family, your church and your community.

In just 41 days you will see a stirring in your life, your faith mature and a life of sacrifice witnessed. In just 41 days you'll begin to deepen your life of generosity.

"How," you ask? Rarely does your generosity motivate others into a personal lifestyle of generosity. As author of this little book, I would like to challenge you, first to be generous by being generous to you. How? Visit us at GenerousLife.net, purchase the book and then begin reading *A Journey to Generosity*. Take a few minutes each day to read the entry and take the challenge. Go ahead; see if the Holy Spirit will deeply change you with each challenge. Then take the ultimate generosity challenge and buy one book for everyone in your family, business and church. Ask them to read it and take the daily challenge....a journey that will deepen their lives and impact their family, their church and their community.

In just 41 days you can see a stirring in their lives, their faith mature and a life of sacrifice witnessed. In just 41 days they can begin to deepen their life of generosity.

~ Mike

Get started today!
AJourneyToGenerosity.com

The best 41 days are ahead!

JOURNEY to Generosity

TAKE THE ULTIMATE CHALLENGE

"In his concise and potent guide to a generous life, Mike Stickler offers a very practical and biblically faithful tour of the fundamental principles of a life that invests in eternity by transmuting the lead of what is passing away into the gold of what will endure forever."

DR. KENNETH BOA
KENBOA.ORG

www.ingramcontent.com/pod-product-compliance
Lightning Source LLC
Chambersburg PA
CBHW072009110526
44592CB00012B/1247